HOW
THE
WORLD
WILL
END

HOW THE WORLD WILL END

BY
DANIEL COHEN

illustrated
with photographs

McGRAW-HILL BOOK COMPANY

New York   St. Louis   San Francisco
Montreal   Panama   Toronto

TO

David MacReynolds

Library of Congress Cataloging in Publication Data
    Cohen, Daniel.
      How the world will end.
      Bibliography: p.
        1.   End of the world.   I.   Title.
QB638.8.C63   909   72-10088
ISBN 0-07-011568-0

CONTENTS

The Sky Is Falling!

Goodness gracious me! said Henny Penny. The
sky's a-going to fall! I must go and tell the king.
—TRADITIONAL ENGLISH FAIRY TALE

Probably the first end-of-the-world panic that any of us ever
heard about was the panic started by Henny Penny in the
old English fairy tale. There are numerous versions of this
story, some gentler than others, but they all make the same
point.

One day Henny Penny gets hit on the head by something. This convinces her that the sky is falling, and she de-
cides she must run off and tell the king. Along the way she
picks up a number of followers, Cocky Locky, Ducky Dad-
dles, Goosey Poosey, Turkey Lurkey, and finally Foxy Woxy.
The whole crowd is going to run and tell the king that the
sky is falling. Just what the king was supposed to do about
this impending catastrophe is never mentioned.

Foxy Woxy tells the others that he knows a shortcut to
the king's palace. He leads them into his cave, where he eats

them all except Henny Penny, who "ran home as fast as her legs could take her; and so she never told the king the sky was a-falling at all."

The moral of this little tale is quite clear. Don't go believing the first person who comes along with a story about the sky falling or anything like that.

Throughout human history there have been people who, like Henny Penny in the fairy tale, have rushed about crying that the sky was falling or that the earth was going to be smashed to bits by a gigantic comet or that California was going to slide into the sea or that something equally catastrophic was just about to happen. There have been many more like Cocky Locky and the rest who have been willing to follow these prophets of doom almost anywhere.

In the chapters that follow we are going to look at the subject of the end of the world from two different angles. First we are going to discuss the Henny Pennys of history, those people who really did believe that the world was just about to come to an end. Why did they hold such beliefs? What happened to them when the world failed to end as predicted?

The subject of end-of-the-world panics is not just a historical one, nor are such beliefs limited to the so-called backward or underdeveloped nations of today's world. Right here in the United States now one can find almost as many prophets of imminent doom as could ever be found in the cities of medieval Europe or in the villages of modern India or Indonesia.

The fear—and the hope—that the whole world will come to a quick and violent end is still very much with us today.

The prophets of doom have been wrong in the past, and they shall be wrong again in the future. But the world is not eternal. It *will* come to an end. That is the second part of the subject that will be examined in this book. How will the world really come to an end?

Of course, we don't know exactly. We have no special revelations, no power of prophecy that will allow us to say that the world will end precisely on such and such a date in such and such a year. We can not even predict what exactly will bring about the final destruction. What we can do is speculate, using the best scientific information available today, as to what the future and final end of the world might be. We offer no predictions, merely possibilities.

The term "the end of the world" itself needs to be defined. What do we mean when we say "the end of the world"? First, and obviously we mean the physical destruction of the planet earth. If the earth suddenly blew up that would be "the end of the world." Even if this catastrophe were to befall the planet earth at some time in the distant future when mankind had already established himself on other planets, the destruction of earth would have to be classified as "the end of the world."

But the earth might physically survive, and the world might still come to an end. If the surface temperature of the earth were raised to 600° F. or the atmosphere evaporated or the planet was subjected to an extended dose of lethal radiation from space or in some other way was suddenly rendered completely unfit for human habitation, that too would constitute "the end of the world."

Thus there are two parts to the problem of the end of the world, the end of our home planet and the end of our species.

For centuries men have wondered and speculated about how the world might end, and they have brought forth many ingenious theories. We will discuss many of these theories. But there are a few ways that the world might end that we will not discuss.

Hostile aliens from another galaxy might suddenly swoop down upon us and wipe us out or eat us or something like that. Such an idea has been the basis for numerous science-fiction stories.

On October 30, 1938, the actor Orson Welles presented a radio broadcast, based on a science-fiction story by the British writer H. G. Wells, called *War of the Worlds*. It was about the invasion of earth by an army of hostile and powerful monsters from Mars. The story was dramatized to sound as if the invasion was actually underway at that moment.

Farmers in the vicinity of the supposed spaceship landing grabbed their guns to defend their lives and property against the "alien invaders." Calls from frightened people poured into police stations, army headquarters, newspaper offices, and radio stations throughout the country. The broadcast had created a real panic.

Obviously, many people really believed that an alien invasion was a possibility in 1938. Today, with the enormous advances in space technology, there are even more people who worry about the possibility of such an invasion. If mankind is reaching out to the planets, why can't creatures from other planets come here?

But such a subject has no place in a book like this. Not because such an invasion could not take place; perhaps it could, perhaps it will. There are more than a few people around who believe or say that they believe that such an invasion is already secretly underway. There is, however, not a shred of evidence to back up such a strange and creepy belief.

Evidence, or lack of it, is the reason we can't discuss the

subject. We simply do not have enough evidence on which we can base any reasonable speculation about an invasion from another world. Most astronomers assume that we do not live on the only planet in the universe upon which life has evolved. Many also speculate that there are other planets in this galaxy or in other galaxies that possess forms of life far more intelligent and advanced than man. But where in the universe might such beings exist? Would they possess the ability to invade the earth? Would they have any reason to invade earth? We simply do not know the answers to any of these questions, and we would be speculating in a vacuum. The entire subject is best left in the realm of science fiction.

Evolution is another subject beyond the limits of this book. We know that species become extinct in nature and are replaced by other species. This may be the ultimate fate of *Homo sapiens*. If the extinction comes on suddenly through some sort of catastrophic change, then we can properly consider such an ending the end of the world. The possibility of the catastrophic extinction of man is discussed in Chapter 6. But if the extinction of man comes about gradually and if man is ultimately replaced by a new species, perhaps evolving out of *Homo sapiens* itself, this is not truly the end of the world. The idea of the end of the world implies that the final act must be sudden, dramatic, and probably violent.

You might wonder why anyone would bother to write about a subject as depressing as the end of the world or read about it, for that matter. But oddly it isn't a depressing subject at all. Rather it possesses a sort of horrifying fascination and even exhilaration.

We have all wondered and even worried about how the world would end. Sometimes we have even hoped that it would end. I can vividly recall times in school when I was facing a test on Friday that I was quite sure I was going to fail. At such moments the thought that the world might end on Thursday was comforting and agreeable. The great catastrophe would put everybody in the same boat and save me from the shame of an individual humiliation.

Speculating about such enormous subjects as the end of the world also gives us a chance to stretch our imaginations to the very limits of human knowledge. This is the most stimulating sort of mental exercise.

Then, as we said, the prophets of doom are still with us today. For reasons that will be discussed later the cries of these prophets will almost certainly become more shrill in the years to come. To review man's past follies about the end of the world, and to understand what may really happen to our world in the future, may save us from becoming the terrified and deluded followers of the next Henny Penny that comes along.

CHAPTER 1

The Midnight Cry

We, while the stars from heaven shall fall,
And mountains are on mountains hurled,
Shall stand unmoved amidst them all,
And smile to see a burning world.

The earth and all the works therein
Dissolve, by raging flames destroyed;
While we survey the awful scene,
And mount above the fiery void.
— FROM A MILLERITE HYMN, 1843

Hardly a year goes by without some well-publicized prediction that the world is about to end. Occasionally one of these prophets of doom attracts a large following, and a genuine end of the world panic is the result. Such an event took place in the northeastern and midwestern United States during the middle of the last century.

The prophet of doom in this case was no silver-throated demagogue or raging fanatic. Rather he was a simple and earnest farmer named William Miller, from Low Hampton, New York, on the Vermont border.

13

William Miller

Like many of his contemporaries, William Miller was a fundamentalist Protestant. He believed in the literal truth of the Bible and in the exact fulfillment of biblical prophecy, and he took his religion very seriously indeed. In about the year 1816 Miller began the self-appointed task of studying his Bible thoroughly so that he would be able to understand all the passages in it, "as to leave me free from embarrassment respecting any mysticism or contradictions."

After two years of farming by day and Bible study by night Miller was convinced that he understood the Scriptures and all their implications. Most significantly he believed that in the course of his studies he had discovered a vital, but hitherto unrevealed message: the end of the world was coming, and it was coming very soon.

He wrote, "I was thus brought, in 1818, at the close of my two years' study of the Scriptures, to the solemn conclusion, that in about twenty-five years from that time all the affairs of our present state would be wound up."

The specific biblical passage which gave Miller his date for the end of the world occurs in Daniel 8:14: "And he said unto me, Unto two thousand and three hundred days; then shall the sanctuary be cleansed."

Miller interpreted the "days" as "years" in the prophecy. Since the prophecy itself was dated about 457 B.C. the end of the two thousand and three hundred "days" would come in about the year 1843. There had been numerous changes in the calendar over two thousand years so Miller was unable to decide on the exact day or even the exact year in which this prophecy would be fulfilled. But he was convinced that the "sanctuary" would be "cleansed" around the year 1843.

The "cleansing" of the "sanctuary" could only mean the purging of the earth by fire—in short, the end of the world, Judgment Day, the Second Advent or Second Coming of Christ was at hand. The trumpets would blow, the sky would roll back to reveal the heavenly host, the graves would give up their dead, and all the righteous would go to heaven, and the sinners would be cast down to hell.

There was nothing at all unusual about Miller's vision of Judgment Day. This vision was shared by all his churchgoing neighbors. Miller, however, was the only one who presumed to know the time when the great and awful event would take place.

Indications that the end of the world was at hand seemed

to come from everywhere. Said Miller, "Finding all the signs of the times and the present condition of the world, to compare harmoniously with the prophetic descriptions of the last days, I was compelled to believe that this world had about reached the limits of the period allotted for its continuance. As I regarded the evidence, I could arrive at no other conclusion."

Somewhat later, and in a more dramatic mood Miller wrote: "Hark!—hear those dreadful bellowings of the angry nations! It is the presage of horrid and terrific war. Look— look again! See crowns, and kings, and kingdoms trembling to the dust! See lords and nobles, captains and mighty men, all armed for the bloody, demon fight! . . . See—see the signs! Behold the heavens grow black with clouds; the sun has veiled himself; the moon, pale and forsaken, hangs in middle air; the hail descends; the seven thunders utter loud their voices; the lightnings send their vivid gleams of sulphurous flames abroad; and the great city of the nations falls to rise no more forever and forever. . . ."

Though Miller was thoroughly convinced that he, and he alone, correctly understood the biblical prophecy of the end of the world he did not immediately rush out to proclaim the truth he had discovered. Quite the opposite, he spent the next fourteen years checking and rechecking his proofs. He studied other prophetic references in the Bible. He made elaborate charts comparing the Hebrew and modern calendars. Everything he did seemed to point to the same conclusion—the world was going to end around the year 1843.

Miller even declined to discuss this belief with his close friends until 1823, when he felt he had overcome all the objections to it that he could think of.

Though, according to Miller, the end of the world was

a mere twenty years hence, his friends and neighbors paid little attention to his predictions in the years following 1823. Miller himself seemed to have neither the ability nor the desire to proclaim his belief to a wider audience.

William Miller did develop a minor local reputation as a good man and a diligent student of the Bible who had arrived at a startling theory about the Second Coming of Christ. In the summer of 1831 Miller was invited to lecture on that subject at a small church in a neighboring town. This was the first public speech Miller had ever made and he was terrified. But he went, and the invitation marked a turning point in his life.

The speech was well-received. Miller was invited to stay on for a week of lectures on the subject of biblical prophecy. The farmer who originally had a fear of public speaking drew courage from this success. In the following months there were more invitations and more lectures.

For the next eight years William Miller devoted an increasing amount of his time and energy to preaching on the subject of the biblical prophecy of the imminent end of the world. He converted many, including some clergymen to his belief, and the term "Millerite" became common in New England and upstate New York. Yet Millerism remained a small and essentially rural movement until 1839. In that year Miller gave his first lecture in Boston. He met and converted to his cause Joshua V. Himes, the pastor of the Chardon Street Chapel in Boston.

Himes was young and vigorous and he possessed an organizational ability and sophistication that Miller entirely lacked. With the addition of Himes, Millerism grew rapidly from a small rural movement to a mass movement involving hundreds of thousands with large groups in most of the cities of the Northeast.

In the summer of 1842 the Millerites held a huge eight-day camp meeting in a grove of hemlocks outside of the little village of East Kingston, New Hampshire. Anywhere from ten to fifteen thousand people traveled to this spot, no easy or cheap trip even by railroad, to hear "Prophet" Miller or "Father" Miller, as he was now called; Himes, and other Millerite leaders lecture and preach, and to engage in almost nonstop prayer sessions.

The time of the end was drawing ever closer. Miller and his followers were becoming increasingly anxious to raise what they called "the Midnight Cry." This phrase came from one of William Miller's favorite Bible stories, Christ's parable of the five wise and five foolish virgins who were waiting for the bridegroom to come for them so that they might go "with him to the marriage." The wait was a long one and they all fell asleep. "And at midnight there was a cry made. Behold, the bridegroom cometh, go ye out and meet him." The wise virgins had brought oil in their lamps and went directly to the marriage celebration. The foolish virgins went out to buy oil, and when they returned they found, "the door was shut." The lesson Christ drew was this: "Watch therefore, for ye know neither the day nor the hour wherein the Son of man cometh." (Matthew 25: 1–13) The Millerites believed that if they did not know the day or the hour, they at least knew the year, and it was their duty to raise "the Midnight Cry."

Miller and his most devout followers needed only their Bibles to convince them that the great and terrible day was nearly at hand. Others looked for signs of the end in the world around them. They found plenty.

In November 1833, when Millerism was first getting started as a movement there was a remarkably bright meteorite shower. Actually meteorite showers occur regularly. This one that took place in November 1833 is part of a series

The great meteor shower of 1833. *Courtesy of the American Museum of Natural History*

known as the Leonid showers, because the meteorites seem to come from the area of the constellation Leo. There had been a spectacular Leonid shower in 1799, and there was to be another in 1866. To many, however, this striking but perfectly natural and regular phenomenon in 1833 seemed a sure sign that the end of the world was near.

On November 25, 1833, a correspondent signing himself "Old Countryman" wrote in the newspaper the *Connecticut Observer:* "We pronounce the raining of fire which we saw on Wednesday morning last, an awful type, a sure forerunner— a merciful sign of the great and dreadful day which the inhabitants of the earth will witness when the Sixth Seal shall be opened. The time is just at hand described, not only in the New Testament, but in the Old. A more correct picture of a fig tree casting its leaves when blown by a mighty wind is not possible to behold." The "Old Countryman's" reference was to the Book of Revelation in the Bible (6:13), "And the stars of heaven fell unto the earth, even as a fig tree casteth her untimely figs, when she is shaken of a mighty wind." This was one of the signs that the end of the world was coming. The "Old Countryman" spoke for many.

As the fateful year of 1843 opened there occurred an even more striking and seemingly unmistakable sign in the heavens. It was the sudden and unexpected appearance of a bright comet.

Nearly forty years after the event this comet was still well remembered. Here is a description of the comet of 1843, written in 1881:

"The Comet of 1843 is regarded as perhaps the most marvelous of the present age, having been observed in the daytime even before it was visible at night—passing very near the sun, exhibiting an enormous length of tail; and arousing interest in the public mind as universal and deep as it was unprecedented. It startled the world by its sudden apparition in the spring in the western heavens, like a streak of aurora streaming from the region of the sun, below the Constellation of Orion. It was first mistaken by multitudes for the zodiacal light, but its aspect and movements proved it to be a comet of the largest class. There were, too, some persons who, without regarding it like many of the then numerous sect called Millerites, as foretokening the speedy destruction of the world, still could not gaze at it untroubled by a certain nameless feeling of doubt and fear. . . . When its distance from the sun allowed it to be visible after sunset, it presented an appearance of extraordinary magnificence."

As an obscure lay preacher with little influence and few followers, William Miller had attracted little attention with his doctrine and therefore little opposition. But as the prophet of a large and ever growing movement, Miller, his followers, and his ideas faced ferocious hostility from many quarters. The scientifically minded found Miller's end-of-the-world theories simply absurd. Ministers denounced his biblical scholarship as simplistic and unsound. But they found, to their great dismay, that large numbers of their parishioners were abandoning established congregations in order to join Millerite groups.

Miller and the Millerite leaders were pictured by their enemies as fanatical madmen who staged hysterical revival meetings and so inflamed their weak-minded followers that many Millerites were actually committed to insane asylums. Others charged Millerite leaders were charlatans who fleeced their deluded followers out of huge sums of money. These charges simply can not be sustained by the evidence.

Neither Miller nor any of his close associates ever became rich from their preaching. Indeed, most of them invested whatever they possessed in the movement. They stuck by their

beliefs in the face of persistent ridicule and crushing disappointment. While many Millerite meetings became quite
emotional, particularly as the predicted end neared, emotional
religious revivals were, and still are, an American tradition.
The only riots that ever took place were those started by the
opponents of Millerism who tried to break up the meetings.
There may have been madmen among the Millerites, but no
more than in the general population.

The bulk of those who followed the movement were
farmers, small-businessmen and laborers, generally from conservative Protestant backgrounds. They were the sort of hard-
working, God-fearing people who were considered the backbone of nineteenth-century America. They in no way differed
from their neighbors, except that they believed that the end
of the world was imminent, while others set it at some in-
definite but hopefully distant date.

What thoughts and emotions drove these thousands of
perfectly ordinary people to the unshakable conclusion that
the world was about to end? The motives are complicated
and doubtless varied greatly from individual to individual,
but here are some of the basic ones:

Paramount, of course, was the belief, common to all
Christians that there will be a Judgment Day. This belief was
particularly influential among fundamentalist Protestants who
interpreted their Bibles very literally. Though the Bible
specifically sets no definite date for Judgment Day, it is
stated quite clearly that the day could come at any time, and
without any warning. Then too there was, and still is, the
belief that certain passages in the Bible provided prophetic
insights into the future if only the passages could be interpreted properly.

But there were other feelings as well. There was strong
belief that the world *should* end. Looking at the world around

"And Fearful Sights and Great Signs shall there be from Heaven."—LUKE XXI. 11.

Falling stars, eclipses, earthquakes and other signs of the Last Days, as depicted in a Millerite publication.

him, the devout Millerite saw it full of sin and wickedness— and he despaired that it could ever be reformed. There was a profound weariness with the day-to-day cares and frustrations of life. Better, the Millerite might think, that the slate should be wiped clean, the sinners punished, and the righteous rewarded. Like all who predict Judgment Day, the Millerites were quite sure that they were the righteous and that they would go to heaven. Those foolish enough not to heed their message or worse yet to make fun of it would burn.

So it was with a sense of joy rather than fear that the Millerites looked forward to the end of the world. The Millerite hymn quoted at the beginning of this chapter pictures the members of the sect ascending to heaven and smiling—yes, smiling—down upon the world aflame beneath them.

The exact date on which the world was to end became an increasing problem for the Millerites. In 1842 a general conference of Millerite leaders passed this resolution:

"*Resolved,* that in the opinion of this conference, there are most serious and important reasons for believing that God has revealed the time of the end of the world, and that that time is 1843."

Thus, at least in the opinion of many of the Millerites the end of the world would come sometime before the end of the calendar year of 1843. At the beginning of that year a rumor of unknown origin swept Millerite groups: the exact date of the Second Coming was to be April 23, 1843. Though the Millerite leaders themselves never accepted this date, and indeed cautioned their followers not to accept it, it seems to have been widely believed.

Miller himself was very wary about setting an exact date. On January 1, 1843, he wrote to his followers:

"I believe that the time can be known by all who desire to understand and to be ready for His coming. And I am fully convinced that sometime between March 21st, 1843, and March 21st, 1844, according to the Jewish mode of computation of time, Christ will come, and bring all his Saints with Him; and then He will reward every man as his work shall be."

When the April 23 date passed without anything unusual happening, the Millerite leaders quite properly pointed out that they had never endorsed that particular date as the one on which the world would end and that the date had been given publicity mainly by their enemies.

When the calendar year of 1843 ended uneventfully, this was a more serious moment of disappointment for the followers of William Miller. But they then recalled the prophet's earlier statement that the critical period could be extended as far as March 21, 1844. This statement had almost been forgotten in the general excitement surrounding the end of the year of 1843.

Though there may have been some disappointment and some defections at the end of 1843, the months between January and March of 1844 actually saw an increase in Millerite activity and a flood of new converts to the ranks.

But when March 21, 1844, came and went without any fresh signs that the world was about to experience the Second Coming, the Millerites faced a real crisis of faith. Their opponents were naturally delighted with the Millerite's discomfort. Clara Endicott Sears, whose book *Days of Delusion* is one of the main sources for information on the movement, described the passing of March 21, 1844, this way:

"The world made merry over the old Prophet's predicament. The taunts and jeers of the 'scoffers' were well-nigh unbearable. If any of Miller's followers walked abroad, they ran the gauntlet of merciless ridicule.

" 'What! Not gone up yet?—We thought you'd gone up! Aren't you going up soon?—Wife didn't go up and leave you behind to burn did she?'

"The rowdy element in the community would not leave them alone."

Miller who had been ill for the early months of 1844 was as puzzled and disappointed as any of his followers. He did not try to excuse his mistaken date, but he did not give up his faith either. On May 2, 1844, the Millerite newspaper printed this statement from their leader:

"I confess my error, and acknowledge my disappointment; yet I still believe that the day of the Lord is near, even at the door; and I exhort you, my Brethren, to be watchful, and not let the day come on you unawares. The wicked, the proud, and the bigot, will exhault over us. I will try to be patient. . . . I want you, my Brethren, not to be drawn away from the truth."

Miller's plea "not to be drawn away" did not go un-

" And I stood upon the sand of the sea, and saw a beast rise up out of the sea, having seven heads and ten horns, and upon his horns ten crowns, and upon his heads the name of Blasphemy."

" And behold a great red dragon, having seven heads and ten horns, and seven crowns upon his heads. And his tail drew the third part of the stars of heaven, and did cast them to the earth."

"And there came out . . . locusts upon the earth
. . . And the shapes of the locusts were like unto
horses prepared unto battle."

"And the fifth angel sounded, and I saw a star
fall from heaven unto the earth: and to him was
given the key of the bottomless pit."

Illustrations of verses from the Book of Revelation that appeared in Millerite publications.

heeded. The movement was at a low ebb in the spring of 1844, but as summer drew on the Millerites, amazingly enough, became more active than ever and more influential. Miller himself, with his health somewhat restored was back on the road preaching to larger audiences. Himes and other leaders extended their preaching activities far into the Midwest, and they were looking beyond the borders of the United States. Wrote Himes:

"If time be continued a few months, we shall send the glad tidings in a number of different languages, among Protestant and Catholic nations. . . .

"A press shall be established at London and lecturers will go out in every direction, and we trust the Word of the Lord will have a free course and be glorified. What we shall accomplish we cannot tell. But we wish to do our duty."

Thus, though the apparent final date set by Miller for the end of the world had irrevocably passed, the movement based on his teachings grew. But the Millerites were unable to exist with the idea that the end of the world would merely be "soon" they needed a definite date and they got one.

As early as February 1844, one of the Millerites, Samuel S. Snow, had put forward the view that the time of the end of the world would be autumn of 1844. On the basis of rather complicated calculations and a generous interpretation of biblical passages, Snow placed the critical date at October 22, 1844. His ideas were forgotten in the general expectation concerning the March 21 date. But with March 21 past, Snow's ideas acquired new importance.

On August 12, there began a major five-day Millerite camp meeting near Exeter, New Hampshire. The meeting had turned into a rather dull affair, and the preachers were barely able to hold the attention of their audience. Then word spread through the meeting that a man with an important message had arrived. Snow had just ridden into the camp. He stepped up to the platform and forcefully delivered his views. Quite suddenly the whole spirit of the meeting changed.

Just a few years after the event, one of those who had attended the camp meeting recalled the electrifying effect Snow's pronouncement had on the Exeter gathering and, shortly after, on the entire Millerite movement:

"There was light given and received there, sure enough; and when that meeting closed, the granite hills of New Hampshire rang with the mighty cry, 'Behold, the Bridegroom cometh, go ye out to meet him!' As the stages and railroad cars rolled away through the different states, cities and villages of New England, the rumbling of the cry was still distinctly heard . . . Time is short! Get ready! Get Ready!"

October 22 is the tenth day of the seventh month, according to the Karaite reckoning of the Jewish sacred calendar, and the movement started by Snow came to be called the "Seventh Month Movement."

Most of the major Millerite leaders at first were taken aback by the unexpected development of this movement within a movement. But one by one they declared for the October 22 date. Miller himself had lingering doubts. He returned to his Bible to recalculate his original prediction and study the October 22 reckoning.

Finally on October 6, just a little more than two weeks before the world was again supposed to end, Miller wrote to Himes:

"I see a glory in the seventh month which I never saw before. Although the Lord had shown me the typical bearing of the seventh month, one year and a half ago, yet I did not realize the force of the types. Now, blessed be the name of the Lord, I see a beauty, a harmony, and an agreement in the Scriptures, for which I have long prayed, but did not see until today. Thank the Lord. . . . I am almost home. Glory! Glory!! Glory!!!"

So it was that Prophet Miller himself was ultimately swept up in the movement that he began, but could no longer control. The Millerite movement from top to bottom became fully committed to the prediction that the world would end on October 22, 1844. There could be no refiguring the date this time.

How did the Millerites face what they fully expected to be the final days of life on this earth? Proper conduct presented something of a dilemma for them. If they were to simply go about their day-to-day activities, they risked being called insincere about their beliefs. On the other hand, if they gave up their jobs and devoted all their energy to preparing for the end, they risked the charge of fanaticism. The Millerites were, by and large, highly conventional and conservative people, and they were very sensitive to the charge of fanaticism.

A Millerite publication recommended a middle course: "We cannot all wholly abstain from labor, but we can imitate the example of a brother in this city, who is a woodsawyer. He said he found that by living temperately he could sustain his body by laboring half a day, and then he could seek for food for his soul the other half."

While some Millerites did sell all or most of their worldly goods usually in order to give money to the movement or to pay outstanding debts that they did not wish to leave unpaid on Judgment Day, most did not take such a radical step.

The period between mid-August and October 22 was one of almost incredible activity on the part of Millerite preachers and lecturers. Camp meetings and other services were con-

tinually jammed, and the Word had been spread far into the Midwest. The presses turned out a steady stream of Millerite publications. Almost no one could escape their message. Even the keepers of isolated lighthouses were not immune, for one of the men whose job it was to provision these outposts was a confirmed Millerite who left a bundle of publications with every delivery of food.

Finally the Great Day had nearly arrived. In a window of a Philadelphia store appeared the following sign:

"This shop is closed in honor of the King of kings, who will appear about the 20th of October. Get ready, friends, to crown him Lord of all."

Just exactly what the Millerites did and did not do on the Great Day has been a matter of some dispute. The popular picture had been that they donned white robes, called ascension robes, and trooped to hillsides or other high places to await the arrival of the Lord with much crying and shouting. There are many stories about Millerites who actually attempted to fly bodily to heaven.

These accounts were collected by Sears:

"One man (I will not use names, as his descendants might not like it), put on turkey wings, got up in a tree and prayed that the Lord would take him up. He tried to fly, fell, and broke his arm. . . . I remember well my father and mother talking about it. I remember hearing them say that some went insane over it."

Or another case:

"When the appointed day arrived a large number of frightened men and women were led by one of the Elders to a spot halfway up a hill outside the city, and under the influence of an abnormal exaltation he was overcome by this same desire to jump into the air which attacked so many. While they were all tremulously looking for the signs of the coming end, and as time went on and nothing happened the tension grew very severe. 'After a long wait,' Mrs. Avery states, 'the Elder, in a white robe, got up on a big stump, and with arms outstretched jumped skyward—but landed on earth. This delusion,' she goes on to say, 'resulted in insanity with many.' "

In a pathetic sort of way, these tales of the Millerites in their white robes trying to fly bodily to heaven and ultimately being carted off to the insane asylum are rather funny, and they have been repeated often. There may have been a few authentic cases which justified such stories, but very few, and they give a false view of the people in the movement. In general, the day the Millerites fervently believed to be the last of the earth's existence was spent calmly in their homes or in the temples they had built. They wore no special robes, and they did not shriek or jump in the air and try to fly. Mostly they prayed or meditated quietly or sang hymns.

The expectations of the Millerites were high as they waited for their "coming Lord until the clock tolled twelve at midnight." Then all true Millerites faced a disillusionment and disappointment of crushing, all-consuming magnitude. Wrote one, "The effect of this disappointment can be realized only by those who experienced it."

Some of the Millerites set down the feelings of the moment:

"Our fondest hopes and expectations were blasted, and such a spirit of weeping came over us as I never experienced before. It seemed that the loss of all earthly friends could have been no comparison. We wept, and wept till the day dawn."

"And now to turn again to the cares, perplexities, and dangers of life, in full view of jeering and reviling unbelievers who scoffed as never before, was a terrible trial of faith and patience."

"Everyone felt lonely, with hardly a desire to speak to anyone. Still in the cold world! No deliverance—the Lord [had] not come! No words can express the disappointment of a true Adventist then. Only those who experienced it can enter into the subject as it was. It was a humiliating thing, and we all felt it alike. . . ."

Millerism had withstood several disappointments regarding the day which the world was to end. But it could not survive this final and greatest disappointment. The world with all its petty cares and troubles was still there. There had been no end and no new beginning. Now the jeering multitudes had to be faced. It is impossible to read the testimony of sincere Millerites at this moment of disappointment without feeling tremendous sympathy for them. But their contemporaries were not all sympathetic. Some who had been members of the movement but now felt betrayed, turned upon it with a particular fury.

Miller again confessed his error about the date and expressed his great surprise and disappointment. But he held fast to the faith that the Second Coming could not be delayed by more than a few months. Indeed, there were numerous ways by which he could have refigured the date, but he did not do so. Miller himself died a sad and broken man in 1849. By that time the faith that had borne his name was virtually extinct.

Some of the former Millerites, now more properly called Adventists, did reinterpret the time of the Second Coming. One group evolved into the sect now called the Seventh Day Adventists, a fairly small but vigorous group. The Seventh Day Adventists do not set an exact date for the Second Coming but they do believe that the time is near. "His Coming, is near, even at the door."

The aggressively proselytizing Jehovah's Witnesses also believe that the world is now in its last days. Indeed, most

fundamentalist Protestant groups share the basic conviction
that the world might end at almost any moment. But few
will follow the lead of the Millerites and try to set an exact
date for the end. Though they believe that the end may be
at hand, they lay great stress on the biblical phrase, "Of that
day or that hour no one knows, not even the angels in heaven,
nor the Son, but only the Father." (Mark 13:32)

CHAPTER 2

Ragnarök and the Apocalypse

The sun turns black, earth sinks in the sea,
The hot stars fall from the sky,
And fire leaps high about heaven itself.
—THE EDDA

Most peoples have developed some pretty definite religious
ideas about how the world was created. But as to how it
would end they were often less clear. Some saw the earth as
eternal, while others saw it going through an endless series
of cycles of death and rebirth. To many the ultimate fate of
the earth seemed a distant and remote concern—one that
they didn't speculate about.

But there were two peoples who developed very dramatic
and convincing pictures of the end of the world, the Christians and the pre-Christian Norsemen. It was the Christian
vision of a great and terrible Judgment Day that moved the
followers of William Miller and, as we shall see shortly, profoundly influenced all Western thinking about the earth, its
past, present and future.

In the Christian vision of the end of the world, of Judgment Day, the earth itself might be purged by fire, but the soul of man and certainly God himself was immortal. To the Norsemen the end of the world was even more complete. In that gloomy religion not even the gods were considered immortal. "The gods are doomed, and the end is death," say the Eddas, the Icelandic poems from which we get the bulk of our knowledge of the religion and mythology of the pre-Christian Norsemen.

The most complete version of the Edda was written down in the twelfth century by the great Icelandic poet Snorri Sturluson. At that time Iceland was nominally a Christian land. But Snorri drew upon the ancient pagan mythology of the Germanic peoples. Other, older versions of the Eddic stories have also been found. The Norse version of the end of the world as it has come down to us was certainly influenced by the Christian idea of Judgment Day, but it has a thundering finality all its own and is worth summarizing.

In the Eddas the end of the world is called Ragnarök, the doom or destiny of the gods. It was called this for the destruction of the world and of the gods was destined since the creation of the world. When Richard Wagner composed his famous operas using the themes from Germanic mythology, he called the end of the world *Gotterdammerung*, or the twilight of the gods. This name was based on a mistranslation, but since "twilight of the gods" sounds more mysterious and alluring (not to mention more hopeful) than "doom of the gods," it has become the more popular phrase.

In the mythology of the Norsemen, men and gods are surrounded by a bewildering and overpowering mass of evil forces, which they can temporarily check, but never overcome. Since both men and gods were imperfect, the time would come when these destructive forces could no longer be kept at bay, and the final, fatal battle would be fought and lost.

There are numerous portents of onrushing disaster throughout the stories of the Eddas, but the incident which really seems to set the final drama in motion is the death of Balder, the blameless son of Odinn, chief of the gods. Balder's death had been arranged through the trickery of the evil and unnatural god Loki. As a punishment Loki is chained beneath a snake which drips horribly painful venom into his face. But this punishment just sets Loki more firmly than ever on the side of the enemies of the gods.

The turmoil among the gods is reflected among mankind which they protect. All restraints between men begin to break down as the end of the world approaches. The entire earth is in an age of warfare, faithlessness, and depravity. "Ax-age, sword-age, storm-age, wolf-age, ere earth is overthrown," say the Eddas.

A brood of monstrous wolves is born in a distant forest in the East. One of these wolves chases the sun. The chase is a long one, but each year the wolf grows in strength and comes closer to the sun, and the summers become shorter and shorter. As the pursuing wolf finally reaches the sun its bright rays are extinguished one by one until it has taken on a blood-red hue and then disappears entirely. Then comes Fimbulvetr, a terrible winter lasting three full years. Snowstorms sweep in from all points of the compass. The whole earth trembles, and all the fetters and bonds that hold the evil creatures of the universe in check are about to snap.

The dramatic, crushing climax now begins. Here is what happens next, as summarized by the scholar Gwyn Jones: "The wolf Fenrir, whose jaws stretch from heaven to earth, breaks his fetters; the Midgard Snake, spewing poison, rises from the sea; Naglfar, the Ship of the Dead, made of the uncut nails of dead men, breaks from her moorings down in Hell. The fire giants, led by Surt, come riding out of Muspell, and as they approach Asgard [home of the gods] the rainbow bridge

An ancient Egyptian representation of the universe. The goddess of the sky, supported by the sun god, arches over the god of the earth. *Yerkes Observatory*

Bifrost cracks under their weight. Giant-home rumbles and the dwarfs whimper. Loki bursts free of his chains and advances to battle."

Heimdall, watchman of the gods blows his horn, and all the gods and chosen heroes gather around Odinn at the Well of Wisdom. According to ancient Germanic custom the opposing armies choose a field of battle. This chosen field for the final battle is Vigird which stretches before Valhalla and is a square measuring a thousand leagues on each side. Though the outcome of the battle is fated, and all the participants know it, all prepare with utmost seriousness. It is a "fight from which none will flee, and none rise up."

The greatest of the gods squares off against the most powerful of the forces of evil. Odinn faces Fenrir. The mon-

Norse view of the universe. Yggdrasill is an ash tree with its roots in the abyss of Hell. Its trunk runs through Midgard, earth, which it supports. The top of the tree issues out of the mountain Asgard, home of the gods.

strous wolf swallows the chief of the gods, but is in turn stabbed by Vidar, Odinn's son. Thor kills the Midgard Snake, but is so filled with the snake's venom that he can walk only nine paces before he dies. Loki and Heimdall kill one another. And so it goes through the list of gods and villains.

With Thor the protector of mankind dead, the human race itself is swept off the surface of the earth. The fire giant Surt sets the earth and heavens aflame. The earth loses its shape, the stars fall out of the sky, and ultimately the entire earth sinks beneath the sea. It is helpful to remember that as far as the Norsemen were concerned, the earth was the center of the universe, and much bigger than the moon or the sun. They also believed that the land of the earth was completely surrounded by a universal ocean. Thus the moon and the sun disappear first, and the final act of the end of the world sequence—the dry land sinking beneath the waves—makes sense in terms of the Norse view of the world.

But the Norse vision of the future does not quite end there. There was to be a rebirth. A new and much better world was to take the place of the old world which had been destroyed.

> In wondrous beauty once again.
> The dwellings roofed with gold.
> The fields unsowed bear ripened fruit.
> In happiness forevermore.

Somehow this vision of a better world reborn is totally unconvincing. The cycle of creation, doom, and rebirth is a common feature in the mythologies of many peoples. The Norse mythology came from this tradition. The Norse, however, spent so much time on the doom part, and their mythology is so gloomy and filled with portents and descriptions of disaster, that the rebirth story reads like it had been tacked on almost as an afterthought, while the Ragnarök part is written with conviction. Says Edith Hamilton, a well-known student of mythology, "This vision of happiness infinitely remote seems a thin sustenance against despair, but it was the only hope the Eddas afforded."

How did the Norsemen live with the dismal prospect of imminent destruction? Did they worry that the world was about to come to an end? Were they ever the prey to end of the world panics? Was there ever a Scandinavian equivalent of William Miller? Could there have been? In truth we know very little about the religious or internal life of the pre-Christian Norsemen. The Eddic poems may not be an accurate reflection of Scandinavian paganism as it really was. Writes Sigurdur Nordal of the University of Reykjavik, "Much of the mythology and many of the stories about the gods are simply the product of the poetic imagination and derive from speculation current during the decline of paganism, occasionally mingled with ideas and motifs that are Christian and southern in origin."

But surely as the Norsemen looked about at their own violent world, at the almost constant wars, the tortures, the murders, the broken treaties and promises, they might imagine that these were the events of the final days predicted in the Eddas. In northern latitudes the winters were so severe anyway that each winter might indeed seem the start of the foretold Fimbulvetr. If a Norseman were so disposed he might believe that "ax-age, sword-age, storm-age, wolf-age . . ." was already upon him, and that it would not be long before "earth was overthrown."

Yet it is doubtful that the Norsemen were much oppressed by the belief that the world was going to end in a violent and horrible way and that there was nothing at all that they could

Illustration of vision from the Book of Revelation. *New York Public Library Picture Collection*

do about it. The Eddas set no definite time for the end of the world. Life had always been hard, violent, and terribly cold. The final age of man's existence might have been going on for thousands of years, and for all anyone knew it could continue for thousands more.

The Norsemen were also an exceptionally vigorous people. Their dragon-prowed ships ranged from the rivers of Russia to the New World and from Byzantium to Greenland. Though they were never numerous, the Norsemen had a tremendous impact on the history of the Western world. They were great sailors, warriors, inventors, artisans, and merchants. Such incessant activity does not seem to be consistent with a people who expected the entire world and all their works to be swept away at any moment.

The Norse were also a practical, realistic, and not terribly religious people who were more concerned with day-to-day life on this earth, which was difficult enough, than with the doings of the gods. There was no powerful priesthood, and the Norse had no particular scruples about neglecting religious obligations. A popular Norse saying was, "Better no prayers than excessive offerings: a gift always seeks a recompense. Better no offering than excessive sacrifice. So declared Odinn before man's memory began." The Norsemen were also fatalists—what would be would be, there was no changing the future, so it was better not to worry about it. The best thing in life was to live and be happy.

The popular maxims of the Norsemen display a cheerful fatalism:

"The lame can ride a horse, a man without hands herd sheep; the deaf can fight and prevail, it is better to be blind than burn [be cremated after death]. A corpse is useless to everyone."

"Praise no day until evening, no wife before her cremation, no sword until tested, no maid before marriage, no ice till crossed, no ale till it's drunk."

These are not the sayings of a people oppressed by end-of-the-world fears. And it is in such maxims, rather than in the grand phrases of the Eddas, that we get a picture of what the people really believed.

While the end of the world might have been of secondary concern to the Norsemen, it was an almost overpowering concern to the early Christians. There were several reasons for this. First, as far as a pagan Norseman was concerned, if the world ended, that was that, and there was nothing he could do about it. He did not have to worry about what was going to happen to his immortal soul. The Christian, however, had to be prepared for the end. He could not sit idly by and wait for it to happen. To do so was to court eternal damnation.

The Norse may have had a casual attitude about their religion, but to the early Christian his religion was the central element of his life. One can hardly imagine one of the early Church fathers saying or even thinking, "A corpse is useless to everyone."

Finally, while the Bible set no date for Christ's return and the end of the world, the earliest Christians certainly believed that this would take place "soon." And "soon" meant within their own lifetime. St. Paul gave this vivid picture of the future:

"The Lord himself will descend from heaven with a cry of command, with the archangel's call, and with the sound of the trumpet of God. The dead in Christ will rise first; then we who remain alive shall be caught up together with them in the clouds to meet the Lord in the air; and so we shall always be with the Lord.

"We shall not all sleep, but we shall all be changed, in a moment in the wink of an eye, at the last trumpet. For the trumpet will sound and the dead will be raised imperishable, and we shall be changed." (I Thessalonians 4:16–17)

Note that Paul speaks of "we who remain alive." Clearly he believed that the great event was to take place within his own lifetime and the lifetime of most of his listeners. In his epistle to the Romans Paul says, "Now is our salvation nearer than we believed." And, "The night is far spent, the day is at hand." (Romans 13:11–12) Examples of this sort are numerous in the New Testament.

The last book of the New Testament, the Revelation of Saint John the Divine (often called the Apocalypse), presents a picture of the end of the world, which makes even the Eddas look tame. The language of this book is the most enigmatic and obscure in the Bible. It has always been the favorite biblical hunting ground for Christian end-of-the-world proph-

The Battle of the Angels from the Apocalypse Series by
Albrecht Durer (1471–1528). *The New York Public Library
Picture Collection*

ets, since the statements it contains can be interpreted in so many different ways.

The Christians, of course, did not invent the apocalyptic vision of the world. Apocalyptic elements can be found in many parts of the Old Testament as well as the New. It was the apocalyptic parts of the Old Testament Book of Daniel that first inspired William Miller's prophecy. Apocalyptic fears and hopes were very much part of the Jewish world into which Christ himself was born. Among the Jews of two thousand years ago there were many who were convinced that something—perhaps the end of the world or the coming of the Messiah—some event of cosmic importance was about to happen. The Jews searched the heavens for comets or other signs of divine favor or disfavor.

The Romans too attached great importance to signs in the sky, but they interpreted them more narrowly. To the Romans a comet might portend disaster for a particular ruler. But to the Jews it could mean only that a worldwide change was forthcoming. Those Jews who converted to Christianity carried their apocalyptic vision with them. Non-Jews who converted to Christianity put less stress on the idea of the Second Coming and more on practical and immediate affairs.

Still the expectation of an imminent end to the world remained a prominent feature of Christianity for a long time. Each generation of Christians grew up believing that theirs was to be the last generation of the world. As the years passed the hold of this idea grew weaker. Around the year A.D. 160 the Christian writer Justian admitted that while he expected the Second Coming of Christ within his own lifetime, not all Christians agreed with him.

The early Church fathers began to move from expectation of an almost immediate Second Advent to the task of building a church organization that would endure until the event.

By the second century of the Christian era it was generally held that the world would end six thousand years after creation. Since the world was then considered to be approximately fifty-seven hundred years old, it could not possibly end for at least another three hundred years, a comfortable length of time.

But the idea that the world was in "the last hour" was so firmly a part of Christian doctrine that there were a number of apocalyptic movements within the early Church and plenty of prophets who found signs of the end in what was happening around them.

As the main body of Christian believers moved toward some sort of an accommodation with this world, there were those who differed radically in eschatological doctrine. "Eschatology" means "the last things," and in Christian doctrine it applied to the plans that the Christians should make for the end of the world.

The movement called Gnosticism, which developed during the first century A.D., held that the world in a sense had already ended, and that life on earth was quite meaningless and unimportant. Gnostics were of two minds as to what to do about this life, in which they were unwillingly imprisoned. Some rejected the world of the flesh entirely and adopted an extremely ascetic mode of living. But another group, believing that since this life had no meaning anyway, abandoned themselves to the most extreme forms of sensuality.

A more conventional apocalyptic movement, Montanism, began in the second century. The movement was started by a recently baptized Christian named Montanus who went into trances and uttered prophecies. He was soon joined by two women, the prophetesses Priscilla and Maximilla, and the three gathered a large following among the Christians of Asia Minor. The Montanists were rigorously ascetic and ac-

Two illustrations from a fourteenth Century German Apocalypse. The end of the world was a favorite theme of Medieval artists. *The Metropolitan Museum of Art, The Cloisters Collection, 1968*

tually sought out martyrdom. The Romans were often happy to oblige them.

Montanists expected the heavenly city of Jerusalem to come down from heaven at a place called Ardabau. This was to be the signal for the Second Coming.

The civil wars that ripped through the Roman world at the end of the second century were viewed by the Montanists as signs of the coming end. In A.D. 198 there was a widespread report that many witnesses had actually seen a walled city in the sky over Judea. It had been seen on forty consecutive mornings. This vision was probably a mirage, and the city was in the wrong place anyway, but to Montanists it could only be the heavenly city descending. But still the end did not come.

Montanism, which had for years been a powerful alternative to orthodox Christianity, went into decline, because it could not adopt to a world that stubbornly refused to end. The doctrines reappeared in one form or another for centuries, but Montanism itself was never again powerful.

Apocalyptic movements were vigorously resisted by the official church, and all who claimed to be able to somehow name the time of Christ's return were condemned as heretical. But still the feeling that the end could come at any moment was so strong that orthodox Christianity has remained a fertile breeding ground for end-of-the-world scares to the present day.

There was one great end-of-the-world scare which was supposed to have overtaken all Christendom as the year 1000 approached. A full millennium after the birth of Christ seemed a proper time to close out the affairs of the world. This particular panic has been described many times. One of the most colorful descriptions was given by Charles Mackay, a nineteenth-century writer who composed a classic work on mass hysteria. To Mackay the panic seemed one of the best historical examples of mass hysteria:

"The scene of the last judgement was expected to be at Jerusalem. In the year 999, the number of pilgrims proceeding eastward, to await the coming of the Lord in that city, was so great that they were compared to a desolating army. Most of them sold their goods and possessions before they quitted Europe, and lived upon the proceeds in the Holy Land. Buildings of every sort were suffered to fall into ruins. It was thought useless to repair them, when the end of the world was so near. Many noble edifices were deliberately pulled down. Even churches, usually so well maintained, shared the general neglect. Knights, citizens, and serfs, travelled eastwards in company, taking with them their wives and children, singing psalms as they went, and looking with fearful eyes upon the sky, which they expected each minute to open, to let the Son of God descend in his glory.

"During the thousandth year the number of pilgrims increased. Most of them were smitten with terror as with a plague. Every phenomenon of nature filled them with alarm. A thunder-storm sent them all upon their knees in mid march. It was the opinion that the thunder was the voice of God, announcing the day of judgement. Numbers expected the earth to open and give up its dead at the sound. Every meteor in the sky seen at Jerusalem brought the whole Christian population into the streets to weep and pray. . . .

"Fanatic preachers kept up the flame of terror. Every shooting star furnished occasion for a sermon, in which the sublimity of the approaching judgement was the principal topic."

This story of the great end-of-the-world panic in the year 1000 has been repeated so often, and in such detail, that it has become one of those "well-known" historical generalities.

But like many other "well-known" historical generalities, this one does not seem to be true.

The first published account of the great panic did not appear until some seven hundred years after the supposed event. There is simply no contemporary evidence that such a panic ever took place. The story really got around during the eighteenth century, and was repeated by such eminent persons as Voltaire and Gibbon. The Middle Ages were in disfavor during the eighteenth century, and many writers were anxious to expose the superstitious and credulous nature of medieval Christians. They seized upon this story of panic because it was useful to their cause and because they believed it. And why not? It sounded, and still sounds, plausible enough—particularly if one doesn't know too much about the Middle Ages.

Historians Jacques Barzun and Henry F. Graff explained that the trained medieval scholar should be able to spot the story as a phony immediately.

"He [the historian] knew in the first place that the end of the world had been foretold so often that only the ignorant in the year of 1000 would seriously believe a new rumor. Moreover, long before that year, it had become orthodox belief and teaching that if the end of the world were really to come no man would know the time in advance."

There were other reasons for rejecting the story. The year 1000 sounds impressive—but in the Middle Ages people used Roman numerals. The year 1000 would have been "the year M." "For the Middle Ages no magic property would attach to 'the year M.' No doubt mystery and significance would then have been connected with 3s, 7s, 12s and their multiples. For these were the sacred numbers of the Jews, and the Christians had repeatedly used them for prophecy."

There was also no generally agreed-upon calendar in

Christian lands. When was the year supposed to begin? In some places the year began at Christmas, in others at Easter, while still other countries used the first of March or the first of September. "In such a state of things the world could obviously not end on schedule everywhere," the scholars comment.

So the great end-of-the-world panic of the year 1000 apparently did not take place, but plenty of smaller ones did and still do. The feeling that the end of the world will come soon is very much a part of our Judeo-Christian heritage. Turn on the radio any Sunday morning and you will hear a host of radio preachers giving bloodcurdling descriptions of the doomsday that is almost upon us and exhorting us to be ready for it.

Even though we may reject many of the specific religious beliefs from which the end-of-the-world fear springs, we cannot escape it. As we shall see, many events, natural events like comets or man-made events like wars, can inspire end-of-the-world fears, and prophets of imminent doom rarely lack an attentive audience.

Nor need one turn back to the history books to find incidents of men and women who were so convinced that the world was about to end that they gave up their normal occupations in order to prepare for it. You need only consult your daily newspaper.

Take this item that appeared in *The New York Times* in January of 1971.

SURVIVAL SHOCKS
APOCALYPTIC SECT
True Lights Thought World
Would End Thursday

CHARLOTTE, N.C., Jan. 2—Leaders of a branch of the True Light Church of Christ, who had taught their 450 followers in North Carolina and South Carolina that the world would end in 1970, said today that they were "surprised" and "shocked" by the failure of the prophecy but not to the extent of doubting any of the sect's other doctrines.

"I can't give you no satisfactory explanation," said H. Flake Braswell, an elder in the sect, who uses the title Temporal Head of Christ's Church. Mr. Braswell said he had not yet decided whether to reopen the upholstery shop near Monroe, N.C., that he closed a year ago in preparation for the end.

He said that several other True Lights who had quit their jobs had told him that they were undecided whether or when to go back to work, Mr. Braswell had estimated last month that 17 members had given up their livelihoods.

The founders of the True Light Church of Christ had arrived at a date for the end of the world, as had William Miller, by study and interpretation of the Bible. The True Lights were heirs to the tradition which held that the world would end six thousand years from the time of Creation. The True Lights placed the date of creation at 4,000 B.C. They also believed that thirty years were lost from the first century of the Christian calendar, and thus the six-thousand-year period was to have ended in 1970.

Not all end-of-the-world prophecies nor even all Christian end-of-the-world prophecies were based solely on biblical study. If the Bible would not reveal the date of the end, then the ancient and distinctly non-Christian practices of astrology and numerology were consulted to set the date. It is ironic that through the Middle Ages, when holders of unconventional ideas were regularly burned as heretics, those who practiced the very pagan arts of astrology and numerology flourished. This in spite of the fact that such practices are specifically denounced in the Bible.

True, an occasional astrologer went too far and offended Church authorities. One named Cocco d'Ascoti was burned at the stake in 1327 for attempting to cast Christ's horoscope. But kings and even popes were deeply influenced by astrologers. At times Church councils were held, not in accordance with Christian tradition, but at times set as favorable by astrologers.

In the year 1179 letters signed by an astrologer named John of Toledo predicted a terrible catastrophe for the year 1186. Not the end of the world perhaps—such predictions were the province of the Church, and to interfere might have been presumptuous and perhaps even dangerous—but a catastrophe that was not far short of the end.

The reason for the astrologer's prediction of disaster was that he had calculated that in the year 1186 there would be a rare conjunction of the planets. In a conjunction the visible planets briefly appear to be at one spot in the sky. We now know that the planets only look as though they are at the same place. In reality they are millions of miles apart. But in 1179 the astrologers really believed that the planets all clustered in a spot in the sky. To the astrologically minded this had to have great significance. The conjunction of 1186 was to take place in the part of the sky which, according to astrological theory was "ruled" by the "stormy" sign of Libra, the scales. A conjunction in such an ominous place could only be a portent of disaster.

A lot of people took this prediction quite seriously and began to prepare as best they could for the natural catastrophe that was about to strike. John of Toledo turned out to be a pretty good astronomer. A conjunction of the planets really did take place in 1186, and to predict one seven years in advance was no mean feat of astronomical calculation in that age. But otherwise he was a poor prophet of doom. The year 1186 passed with no more than the usual number of disasters. Later word got around that the prediction had not really been wrong, but that it had been symbolic. John of Toledo, it was said, was not referring to a real natural catastrophe but to the invasion of barbarians. Since barbarian invasions had been going on regularly for hundreds of years, this was a very safe prediction.

Even today a conjunction of the planets is likely to set off a flurry of end-of-the-world rumors among the astrologically minded. A rare conjunction of five planets took place on February 5, 1962. In some parts of the world, like Ceylon and Indochina, where astrology has a powerful grip upon public imagination, there were some end-of-the-world predictions reported. In the United States, where astrology is currently enjoying a great rebirth of interest, astrologers were much more cautious. They predicted that "something" important would happen, though they were not very specific about what that "something" might be. As it turned out February 5, 1962, was a pretty ordinary day. Were the astrologers and their followers shaken by this? Not at all. Many blandly asserted that "something" had indeed happened, but that we should not see the results of that "something" for many years to come.

The celebrated fifteenth-century English prophetess Mother Shipton predicted that the world would end in 1881. Mother Shipton had a reputation for uncanny accuracy. This is hardly surprising. In the first place there probably never was a Mother Shipton. Most of her "prophecies" were written up after the prophesized event had taken place. They were then supposedly "discovered" in an "old manuscript" by an enterprising publisher who put out a highly successful volume on Mother Shipton in the nineteenth century. The 1881 prediction obviously did not come off. Fortunately, by that time the Mother Shipton hoax had been thoroughly exposed, so the "prediction" set off no panic.

Predicting the future has always been an uncertain business. But we can confidently predict an ever increasing volume of end-of-the-world predictions between now and the year 2000. Perhaps the year 1000 meant little to men of the Middle Ages, but the year 2000 means a great deal to modern numerologists, who believe that there is an overpowering significance to certain numbers and dates. Already there have been numerous predictions that "something," a great war, a great religious revival, perhaps something as catastrophic as the end of the world will take place in that year.

CHAPTER 3

The Deluge and Atlantis

> And every living substance was destroyed which
> was upon the face of the ground, both man and
> cattle, and the creeping things, and the fowls of
> heaven; and they were destroyed from the earth;
> and Noah only remained alive, and they that were
> with him in the ark.
>
> —GENESIS 7:23

What we believe is going to happen in the future is profoundly influenced by what we think has already happened
in the past. One of the primary reasons that men were so
convinced that the world would end catastrophically was
their belief that a similar catastrophe had already occurred.
For centuries almost everybody in the Western world, from
the simplest peasant to the most learned scientist, knew that
the world had already ended at least once and perhaps several times.

The story of the universal flood and of Noah's ark is
one of the most dramatic and best known parts of the Bible.
While the origins of many of the events described in the

Bible remain obscure, the origins of the flood story are surprisingly well known.

The story of the flood has been traced back to the Gilgamesh Epic, the oldest piece of literature that survives. It is at least six thousand years old. The Gilgamesh Epic was first written down in the valley of the Tigris and Euphrates rivers, in what is now Iraq, by the Sumerians. The Sumerians were, as far as we know, the world's first civilized people. They set the pattern followed by all of the other civilizations of the ancient Middle East. One of the most influential and unexpected legacies of this ancient people is the story of the flood.

Bits and pieces of the Gilgamesh Epic appear in the writings of several ancient Middle Eastern civilizations. Each group adapted the story slightly, inserting the names of its own heroes and gods. The most complete existing copy of the epic was found inscribed on clay tablets in the library of the Assyrian king Assurbanipal at Nineveh. In this version there appears the story of the faithful Utnapishtim who is warned by the gods of the coming flood.

Utnapishtim is commanded to build a ship and save his family and representatives of the game and beasts of the field from destruction.

The parallels between the story of Utnapishtim and the flood and the biblical story of Noah and the flood are undeniable. The Hebrews had probably picked up the flood story during the time of the Babylonian captivity.

But where had the flood story come from originally? Had it simply been the product of some Sumerian poet's imagination, or had it been inspired by a real event? Archeologists believe that they have found clear evidence of a very real catastrophe, one that has left a lasting impression on the minds of men.

Noah builds the Ark. From a late fifteenth century woodcut.
Courtesy the Walters Art Gallery

In the 1920s the great British archeologist Sir Leonard Woolley was conducting excavations in the valley of the Tigris and Euphrates. He was digging at the city of Ur, known in the Bible as Ur of the Chaldees, home of the Hebrew patriarch Abraham. The city had existed long before the time of the Chaldeans or of Abraham. It had been founded first by the Sumerians.

Woolley was trying to determine how far back the civilization of Ur went. He had his workmen sink a five-foot square shaft. They dug through layer after layer of brick, broken pottery, and other debris—all evidence of human habitation. Then abruptly the layers of debris ceased. The diggers had reached a layer of clean clay. They reported that since there were no more signs of human habitation there was no need to dig any deeper.

Woolley was inclined to agree, but it seemed that the evidence of human occupation did not go back nearly as far as he had expected. There was something wrong. On a hunch he ordered his diggers to continue. They did, though they clearly indicated that they thought it was all a waste of time.

After digging through eight feet of clean clay, the workmen reached a layer of soil which contained broken pottery, flint implements, and other unmistakable signs of the presence of man. People had lived at Ur in very early times. Then something had happened that broke the continuity of life at Ur. Only after a long period did men return to the city. The thick layer of clay could only have been laid down as silt by a tremendous quantity of water.

When Mrs. Woolley looked at the excavation she said aloud what everybody else had been thinking, "Of course, it's the flood."

Such a startling conclusion needed more support than what could be found in one single five-foot square shaft. Woolley set his diggers to work in other spots around Ur, and everywhere they found the layer of clean water-laid clay. Signs of human habitation appeared both above and below the clay. The deepest layer of clay discovered was eleven feet. Woolley estimated that this indicated a flood of no less than twenty-five feet. In Genesis 7:10 it states, "Fifteen cubits upward did the waters prevail." Fifteen cubits is approximately twenty-five feet.

According to Woolley's calculations, the flood that created the layer of clay at Ur must have covered an area three hundred miles long and one hundred miles wide. This would have submerged the entire Tigris and Euphrates valley. The valley contains no natural hills to which the inhabitants could have fled for protection. Only the higher parts of cities which were built on artificial mounds might have provided some refuge from the waters. The valley of the Tigris and Euphrates must have experienced floods regularly in ancient times, but there was nothing to compare with this catastrophe.

Wrote Woolley, "It is not a universal deluge, it was a vast flood in the valley of the Tigris and Euphrates which drowned the whole habitable world between the mountains and the desert; for the people who lived there, that was all the world.

"The great bulk of these people must have perished, and it was but a scanty and dispirited remnant that from the city walls watched the flood recede at last. No wonder that they saw in this disaster the gods' punishment of a sinful generation, and if some household had managed to escape by boat from the drowned lowlands the head of it would naturally be chosen as the hero of the saga."

This story of this ancient catastrophe was passed on from generation to generation. It was to have profound and quite unexpected effects upon the minds of men for thousands of years.

Throughout most of the Christian era most people in Europe believed that the whole world had once been covered by a great flood just as described in Genesis. Why shouldn't people have believed in the flood? The Bible was the only book that they ever read, or more likely had read to them, for most people could not read at all.

The idea that everything in the Bible had to be interpreted literally was not nearly as important in the early days of Christianity, as it was to become later. No one seriously challenged the Bible so it did not have to be defended as

vigorously. St. Augustine (A.D. 354–430) certainly did not
interpret the Bible literally, nor did the two great Christian
scholars of the thirteenth century, St. Thomas Aquinas and
St. Albertus Magnus. Throughout much of the Middle Ages
the views of the ancient Greek philosopher and natural scientist Aristotle (384–322 B.C.) about the nature of the world
were almost as influential as the ideas expressed in the Bible.
Aristotle held no catastrophic view of earth history. He saw
our planet as a place of constant, but slow and undramatic
changes.

"The distribution of land and sea in particular regions
does not endure throughout all time," Aristotle said, "but it
becomes sea in those parts where it was land, and again it
becomes land where it was sea. . . . As time never fails, and
the universe is eternal neither the Tanais nor the Nile can
have flowed forever. . . . So also of all other rivers; they
spring up, and they perish; and the sea also continually deserts some lands and invades others. The same tracts, therefore, of the earth are not some always sea and others always
continents, but everything changes in the course of time."

By the late sixteenth century it was the Bible and not
Aristotle that provided the final word on the earth's past,
present, and future. To oppose a strict interpretation of the
Bible might be dangerous, indeed it might be fatal. In 1632
Galileo was forced by the Inquisition to publically disavow
his stated belief that the earth revolved around the sun. The
newly rising Protestant churches were if anything, more in-
sistent on a strict literal interpretation of the Bible, than the
Catholic church ever was. In this atmosphere the flood of
Noah's time was an unquestioned truth. It was soon to grow
into an obsession.

In the seventeenth century two formidable challenges
to Christian orthodoxy were raised. Scholars, most of them

churchmen, had begun to study the original sources of the Bible. They found many changes in interpretation, many gaps, and out-and-out mistranslations. Perhaps the literal truth of the Bible could not be relied upon after all.

An even more serious challenge was presented by the growing interest in the physical sciences. The world being uncovered by science was one ruled by "natural" often mathematical laws. It was a world which left no room for revealed truth. Nor did science allow for miracles, rather it sought to explain "miracles" in natural terms.

The story of the flood seemed to provide a unique opportunity to silence the critics of religion and reestablish the primacy of the Bible, though on a new basis. First, if the flood could be proved to be historically true, this would show that the Bible was no mere collection of primitive fables. Secondly, if the flood could be used to explain scientifically many of the puzzling things that were being discovered about the earth, then science and religion would be allies not enemies. Some hoped that a new sort of Christianity could be built with its authority resting on scientific fact and not revelation.

Numerous attempts were made to provide a natural or scientific explanation for the flood. One of the problems was figuring out where all the water had come from, and what had happened to it after the flood receded. It was not good enough simply to say that God created the water for the flood, and when the flood was over He annihilated the extra water. Such simple explanations no longer satisfied the science-minded gentlemen of the seventeenth century.

A noted English cleric named Thomas Burnet (1635–1715) came up with a unique theory about the flood. According to Burnet, when the earth was created out of chaos it formed into three layers. The first two layers were a solid heavy inner core and a surrounding layer of water. Dust and other particles, the debris of the Creation, floated above the water and slowly settled on the surface. These solid particles mixed with the "oily liquor" and eventually hardened into a thick smooth skin, the crust of the earth. It was an earth without mountains and without seas. This dull and featureless globe that resembled a billiard ball possessed, in Burnet's view, the "smooth beauty of youth" and was "well suited to a golden age."

But the sun beat down on the new earth causing the surface to crack and heating the waters that lay below. Finally, at a time chosen by God to punish a sinful people, the waters gushed forth from the cracks. "The whole fabric broke and the frame of the earth was torn into pieces, as by an earthquake." A mighty wave swept across the surface crushing everything in its path—this was the universal deluge.

What about the forty days of rain? Why had Noah not noticed that the water was coming from below the surface of the earth and not falling from the sky? The answer to that was found in Genesis 8:13: ". . . and Noah removed the covering of the ark, and looked, and, behold, the face of the ground was dry." During the time of the deluge the ark had been covered, so Noah could not know where the water was coming from and simply assumed it was falling from the sky.

What was left of the earth after the deluge in Burnet's view was "a ruine." All the major features of the earth, the mountains, seas, and continents were products of the collapse of the original smooth crust of the earth during the disaster.

The flood seemed to explain admirably yet another puzzling thing about the earth, the existence of fossils. Since the days of the cavemen, people had been finding objects that looked like shells or bones made out of stone. Other stones seemed to contain the picture or impression of a plant or animal. Often the fossilized remains of sea creatures were found high on mountains or far inland where there was no water.

Back in the third century A.D. the Christian thinker, Tertullian, had suggested that fossils were relics of the flood. But at that time the problem of fossils was not an important one and the suggestion was forgotten. In the fifteenth century that universal genius Leonardo da Vinci had correctly deduced the nature of fossils. But a century after Leonardo most educated people refused to believe that fossils were the remains of living things. It seemed inconceivable that living things could be turned to stone. Many in the West followed the lead of the great Arab thinker Avicenna (980–1037) who said that fossils were the result of a *vis plastica,* a sort of natural shaping force. Others thought that fossils were mere "sports of nature." It wasn't until the seventeenth century that people generally recognized that fossils were indeed the remains of living creatures. By that time the flood was not merely a convenient way to explain the existence of fossils, it was a necessary one.

Those who believed that the earth had been swept by a universal deluge were called *diluvialists.* The world that had existed before the flood was the *antediluvian* world.

One enthusiastic diluvialist was a Swiss named Johann Jacob Scheuchzer (1672–1733). He published a description of a fossil which he believed to be "the bony skeleton of one of those infamous men whose sins brought upon the world the dire misfortune of the deluge." Scheuchzer named the fossil *Homo diluvii testis* ("man witness of the deluge"). This particular fossil was about a yard in length and it showed clearly a head and backbone. But the resemblance of this skeleton to a human skeleton was slight. Within a century

Scheuchzer's "deluge man" was correctly identified as a giant salamander. To Scheuchzer, salamanders were little things that could fit in the palm of the hand. The idea that a giant salamander might once have existed never occurred to him. The salamander was later given the scientific name *Andrias scheuchzeri*, in Scheuchzer's honor. It was an ironic tribute.

Scheuchzer published his description of the "deluge man" in 1726, but he did not date his publication with that year. So convinced was he of the reality of the flood that he dated his book "In the Year (4032) after the Great Flood." Not only had Scheuchzer put a year on the flood, he even thought that he knew the season of the year in which it had taken place. From the "tender, young, vernal" state of some seed cones Scheuchzer concluded that the flood occurred in May. A contemporary disagreed. The flood, he said, had taken place in the fall and this was proved by the number of "ripe" fruits found among the fossils.

Some scholars turned their attention to Noah and his ark. How, they wondered, had Noah been able to squeeze two representatives of all the living creatures in the world aboard a single boat. One of those who thought most seriously about this subject was Father Athanasius Kircher, S.J. (1601–1680), an immensely learned man, gifted or perhaps cursed with a too vivid imagination. Father Kircher wrote about many things—the origins of dragons and the conditions on other planets, and in 1675 he wrote a book about Noah's ark. He listed all the animals that were admitted to the ark, "and therefore did not perish in the Flood." He even described the ark and the cages in which the different animals were kept.

Father Kircher's "scientific ark" was a boxlike affair, with three hundred stalls on the first deck, a granary on the second, and space for two thousand cages and Noah's family on the third. This attempt to figure out a cargo arrangement for Noah's ark sounds fantastic and foolish to us today. But we should not judge the beliefs of the seventeenth century by the standards of the twentieth. Father Kircher was no fool. He simply lived at a time when the idea of the universal deluge was accepted by almost everyone, and seemed to be supported not only by Scripture but by observable evidence—the fossils of sea creatures found far from the sea.

In one way at least Father Kircher was quite advanced for his time. He admitted the possibility that there were animals that had not been able to get into the ark—that there were extinct species. For a long time people did not believe that entire species could become extinct. President Thomas Jefferson, who usually reflected the enlightened opinion of his day put his belief thus: "Such is the economy of nature that no instance can be produced of her having permitted any one race of her animals to become extinct; of her having formed any link in her great work so weak as to be broken."

Jefferson himself was a keen amateur scientist. He did a lot of digging around his own estate in Virginia, and he came up with the bones of elephantlike creatures that clearly no longer lived in Virginia or anywhere else so far as he knew. But Jefferson could not believe that such creatures were extinct. Rather he thought that they still lived somewhere, perhaps in the vast unexplored western part of America.

But as more and more fossils were discovered it became overwhelmingly obvious that there were an enormous number of animals that no longer lived anywhere on this earth. So numerous and so striking were these extinct creatures that it was not possible to consider them as simply a few animals that had "missed the ark." Also it was becoming clear that these different animals had lived at different periods in the history of the earth. A Swiss naturalist by the name of Charles Bonet (1720–1793) popularized the idea that the world had been swept by periodic catastrophes, of which the biblical flood was only the latest.

The theory of periodic catastrophes was adopted by the most imposing scientific figure of the early nineteenth century, George Léopold Chrétien Fréderic Dagobert Baron de Cuvier (1769–1832). No man in history has ever been a finer or more accurate observer of fossils. Baron Cuvier almost singlehandedly created the science of paleontology. His prestige in the scientific world was enormous, too great in fact for the good of science. Cuvier became the virtual dictator of the biological sciences in Europe. If Cuvier said that the world had been swept by successive catastrophes, then that was what must have happened. Few scientists disagreed publicly with Cuvier, and those who did usually regretted it. Cuvier was a formidable and ferocious opponent.

Just exactly what Cuvier believed about these catastrophes is not entirely clear. Many of his followers unhesitatingly declared that the world had ended catastrophically many times. A favorite idea was that there had been six ends to the world, for this tallied nicely with the biblical six days of Creation. In each of these catastrophes all of life was destroyed and there was an entirely new Creation. The fossils were the remains of creatures killed off in past catastrophes.

Cuvier himself did not go quite this far. He seemed to believe in restricted catastrophes that killed off all the creatures in one part of the world but did not destroy all life on earth. On the other hand he never specifically rejected the idea of the complete end of all life followed by a new Creation. Though he was very definite about most subjects, Baron Cuvier had probably not made up his mind about this one.

One thing Cuvier had very definitely made up his mind about, however, was that all the living things, past and present, had been created in their finished form and that there was no such thing as evolution. When Cuvier died in 1832 he was only sixty-three years old and up to the last day of his life he had seemed in perfect health.

In 1832, Cuvier was at the height of his powers and influence, and his death came as a surprise and shock to the scientific community. Many considered Cuvier's untimely death a tragedy. But perhaps Cuvier was lucky, for within a very few years all his views about catastrophes and creation of life were overturned by new discoveries. A succession of geologists proved that most of the earth's features had been formed slowly over a long period of time. They could find no evidence of regular catastrophes. Ultimately Charles Darwin provided believers in evolution with the theory and the facts to win their case against the followers of Cuvier's catastrophism. Despite the enormous contributions that Cuvier really did make to science he is remembered primarily as a man who was wrong about evolution.

Today, science rejects the idea that the entire world was overwhelmed by regular catastrophes like universal floods. (Though as we shall see in Chapter 5, some scientists think that there have been worldwide catastrophes of a type that Cuvier had never dreamed.) Most religious leaders accept the idea that the story of the flood of Noah was drawn from experience with a catastrophic flood in the Tigris and Euphrates valley and not with a universal deluge.

Yet the idea of past catastrophes has not lost its appeal for the general public. Books of theories by "cataclysmists" or "catastrophists" still appear regularly. Those who try to prove that the earth has been destroyed in the past are very nearly as popular as the prophets who predict that the earth will be destroyed in the near future.

The forty days and forty nights of rain. From a late fifteenth century woodcut. *Courtesy the Walters Art Gallery*

Here is a composite picture of a modern catastrophist. He is usually an energetic and well-educated man, but not a man trained in geology, paleontology, or any of the other sciences relevant to uncovering the past history of the earth. The catastrophist draws support for his theories from a huge variety of sources, myths and legends, archeology, paleontology, astronomy, etc. But he picks only those bits of evidence which support his beliefs and ignores all contradictory evidence. Very often the catastrophist relies on dubious theories, mistranslations, or simply misinterprets the evidence to suit his own beliefs.

It would be a mistake, however, to put down the modern catastrophist as a fraud, a fool or a madman. Usually he is honest, intelligent, and quite sane—he is simply devoted to an incorrect idea. Often the catastrophist is driven by the desire to prove that the Bible or parts of it are literally true, though he may not easily acknowledge or even understand the emotional basis of his beliefs.

Why are catastrophists eternally popular with the general public? There are several reasons. As we have already pointed out the idea that the world has undergone and will continue to undergo enormous catastrophes is an ancient and deeply ingrained one. Catastrophes simply make sense to a lot of people, whereas slow processes like erosion and evolution do not. It is hard to think in terms of millions of years.

The catastrophist can write broadly and dramatically about grand themes like universal floods and world-shaking earthquakes. The arguments of geologists and paleontologists are dull by comparison. Often the scientific arguments are technical or even mathematical and thus not easily understood by the general public.

Finally the catastrophist usually roundly denounces the scientific "establishment" as being blind, pigheaded, and prejudiced against anyone who is not a member of that establishment. The catastrophist thus presents himself as sort of a martyr, or at least an underdog, being either persecuted or ignored by this vast and closed scientific establishment. Anyone who feels persecuted, pushed around, and ignored (and who doesn't) may respond sympathetically to such an underdog. Besides we all like to see the high and mighty get knocked off their pedestals once in a while. And if the high and mighty scientists could be proved to be wrong about the history of the earth, that would be quite a come-uppance.

The most active and influential catastrophist of the last hundred years was Ignatius Donnelly (1831–1901). Donnelly was a lawyer from Minnesota who, at the age of twenty-eight was elected lieutenant governor of the state. He later spent eight years in the House of Representatives in Washington, helped to found the Populist party and ran twice for Vice President on its ticket. But he is best remembered for his strange theories which earned him the title of "America's Prince of Cranks."

While in Washington Donnelly's duties were not too arduous, and he put in many hours at the Library of Congress, soaking up information on a variety of subjects and becoming perhaps the most well-read man ever to sit in Congress. Donnelly wrote a book called, appropriately enough, *Ragnarök*, which detailed the successive catastrophes which he believed had swept the earth. Scientifically his theories were nonsense, but they were very popular in their day, and even now Ignatius Donnelly's strange books have a wide readership.

More recently a psychiatrist named Immanuel Velikovsky put forward a series of catastrophic theories, which created a genuine popular controversy in the 1950s. But we

HOMO DILUVII TESTIS.

Bein-Gerüst/

Eines in der

Sündflut ertrunkenen

Menschen.

Wir haben/ nebst dem ohnfehlbaren Zeugnuß des Göttlichen Worts/ so viel andere Zeugen jener allgemeinen und erschrecklichen Wasser-Flut/ als viel Länder-Stätte Dörffer/ Berge/ Thäler/ Stein-Brüche/ denn Zeugen sind. Pflanzen/ Fische/ vierfüssige Thiere/ Ungeziefer-Muscheln/ Schnecken/ ohne Zahl/ von Menschen aber/ so demahls zu Grund gegangen hat man biß dahin sehr wenig Ueberbleibsel gefunden. Sie schwimmen tod auf der obern Wasser-Fläche/ und verfaulten/ und läßt sich von denen hin und wider befindlichen Gebeinen nicht allezeit schliessen/ daß sie von Menschen seyen. Dieses Bildnuß/ welches in saubern Holtz-Schnitt der gelehrten und curiosen Welt zum Nachdencken vorlege/ ist eines von sicherlich ja ohnschwerer Ueberbleibsel der Sünd-Flut/ da finden sich nicht einige Lineament/ auß welchen die reiche und fruchtbare Einbildung etwas/ so dem Menschen gleichet/ formieren kan/ sondern eine gründliche Uebereinstimmt/ mit denen Theilen eines Menschlichen Bein-Gerüsts/ ein vollkommenes Eben-Maaß/ ja selbs die in Stein (der auch dem Oninger Stein-Bruch) eingenckete Bein/ selbs auch weichere Theil sind in Natura übrig/ und von übrigem Stein leicht zu unterscheiden. Dieser Mensch/ dessen Grabmahl alle andere Römische und Griechische auch Egyptische/ oder andere Orientalische Monumente an Alter und Gewißheit übertrifft/ präsentiert sich von vornen. A B C. ist der Umbfang des Stirn-Bauns (alles in natürlicher Grösse) B. die Mitte der Stirn. A. das rechte Joch-Bein. C. das linde. D E G H. die Augenliesen. K L. die Dicke des Stirn-Beins mit dessen beyden Tafeln/ der äusseren und inneren. M. das Loch der unteren Augenliese/ welches die Sehn-Ader des fünfften Nerven hindurchläßt. N. Sind Reliquien von dem Gehirn/ oder des harten Hirn-Häutleins. O. Die Gebein/ welche die Augenlieslen formieren. P. Die Siebförmigen und schwammichen Bein. P Q. Die Pflug-Schar/ so durch die Mitte der Nasen herunter gehet. U. Ein ziemliches Stück vom rechten Backen-Bein. W. Scheinet seyn ein Stuck des Stirn-Muskuls. X. Ueberbleibsel der Nasen. Y. Ein Stuck vom säulenden Muskul. B C. Ein Durchschnitt von dem untern Kiefel wie der von dem dickeren Fortsatz gehet zu dem untern Eck oder Winckel. D. Stücker vom untern Kiendbaken gegen dem Kien. 1. 2. 3. &c. biß 16. und 16. Auf zwei Wirbel/ namlich 6. vom Hals/ und 10. vom Rucken/ da gemeinlich die Nebenfortsätze bloß ligen. 11. Ein Stuf vom Radenförmigen Fortsatz des Schulter-Blatts. C H. Ein Stuck vom ersten Ripp/ welches annoch mit Stein überzogen. z. Ueberbleibsel von der Leber. Auß der gantzen Grösse läßt sich schliessen/ in Gegenhalt der übrigen Theilen/ daß die Höhe dieses Menschen steiget auf 58½ Pariser Zoll welche entsprechen 5. Zürcher Schuhe 9¾. Decimal Zoll.

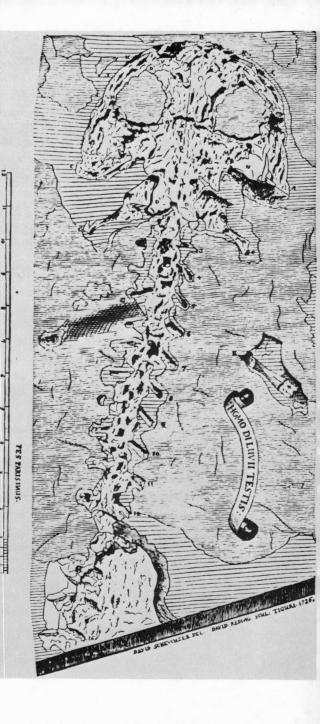

Joh. Jacobi Scheuchzeri,
Med. D. Math. P.

David Reding/ Formschneider.

Im Jahr nach der Sündflut
MMMM XXXII.

TES PARISINUS.

DAVID SCHEVCHZER DEL   DAVID REDING SCUL. TIGURI. 1726.

will hear more of Dr. Velikovsky and his ideas in a later chapter.

While some still attempt to prove that the world once ended in the great flood, there are others who search for the remains of Noah's ark. From time to time, someone, somewhere announces that he has found the remains of the ark.

Most recently a group sponsored largely by the fundamentalist Seventh Day Adventists announced that they had found the remains of a massive ancient wooden structure that might be the ark beneath a glacier on Mount Ararat in Turkey. Mount Ararat is one of the highest and most inhospitable mountains in the biblical world. According to the book of Genesis, Noah's ark landed on "the mountains of Ararat."

The find on Mount Ararat was originally made in 1955 but little has been said about it publicly. To the time of this writing what exactly has been found and where is not at all clear. Pieces of wood found on the mountain and supposed to be timbers from the ark have been analyzed by the radio-carbon dating process. The wood seems to come from a tree that grew in A.D. 600. The biblical flood would have to have taken place several thousand years earlier. Still the finding of any sort of man-made structure high on Mount Ararat has come as a surprise.

Next to the flood, the most widely discussed ancient catastrophe was the one which supposedly resulted in the sinking of the "lost continent" of Atlantis. Many say that the Atlantis story began with the flood or vice versa. There is no need to reexamine the entire Atlantis controversy here. The subject has inspired thousands of books in dozens of languages. Any good library can supply at least one and probably a score or more of books on the subject of Atlantis.

This fossil, first identified as a man drowned in the Deluge, turned out to be a giant salamander.

A modern deluge at Fairbanks, Alaska, in 1967. *Daily News —Miner* photo from the American Red Cross

We will give the tangled history of the "lost continent" only in barest outline. The story begins with the Greek philosopher Plato. Around the year 355 B.C. Plato wrote a series of dialogues in which he recounts the founding, growth, and destruction of a large island in the Atlantic ocean, beyond the Pillars of Hercules, or Straits of Gibraltar. The island was called Atlantis.

According to Plato, Atlantis once was the home of a high civilization and the people there lived in sort of a golden age. But they became greedy and insolent and their homeland was destroyed by flood and earthquake in "one terrible day and night. . . ." Plato also mentions his belief that the world was swept by periodic catastrophes, and that the destruction of Atlantis was part of one of these catastrophes.

Most of Plato's contemporaries, including his famous student Aristotle, regarded the story of Atlantis as a fable. However, a thousand years or so after Plato died some writers began to think of the story of Atlantis as true history and not a fable at all. Medieval cartographers often put a large island in the middle of the Atlantic and called it Atlantis. But medieval cartographers customarily dotted the unknown ocean with imaginary islands.

The search for the "lost continent" has been conducted in all parts of the world. Atlantis has been "located" in such unlikely places as the North Sea and the middle of the Sahara desert! In 1882 the energetic Ignatius Donnelly wrote a book on Atlantis. This book remains the bible for all pseudo-scientific Atlantis hunters.

In 1967 a group of Greek and American scientists announced that they had discovered what they believed to be the inspiration for Plato's Atlantis story. They found evidence that in the fifteenth century B.C. a volcano called Santorini in the Aegean sea near Greece erupted violently. The eruption of Santorini seems to have been one of the biggest and most destructive volcanic explosions since man has inhabited the earth. As a result of the explosion a large part of an island now called Thera sank into the sea. Thera was inhabited by a people called the Minoans, whose civilization was centered on the nearby island of Crete. The early Greeks were barbarians compared to the Minoans and had learned much from them.

The ash from the Santorini explosion may also have fallen heavily on Crete itself and disrupted life on the island. Minoan civilization went into a puzzling decline about the time of the explosion. There is even a theory that the Santorini eruption was the inspiration for some of the biblical descriptions of the awesome events surrounding the exodus of the children of Israel from Egypt. The "plague of darkness" which the Bible says occurred at the time of the exodus may have been caused by the volcanic cloud.

More than two thousand years after Plato first wrote of Atlantis, the controversy surrounding it is still very much alive. But even if the Santorini explosion was the source of Plato's Atlantis story (and we probably will never know for sure) it was not the sort of universal catastrophe that could bring the world to an end.

The Atlantis story is also closely tied to modern end-of-the-world fears. The idea has gotten around that the sunken island-continent of Atlantis will someday, somehow, rise again and that this rising will mark the beginning of vast worldwide cataclysms, perhaps the end of the world itself. No modern mystic prophet worth his salt has failed to predict the rising of Atlantis and attendant cataclysms in the rest of the world. Some people now believe that the rising of the "lost continent" has begun.

The seed for the current crop of fears about the rising of Atlantis and the end of the world was planted in the 1930s and 1940s by Edgar Cayce, a mystic healer who oper-

ated out of Virginia Beach, Virginia. People would come to
Cayce with their medical problems. He would lie down on
a couch and presumably fall asleep. While asleep he would
diagnose his "patients'" illness. By such methods Cayce
achieved a moderate degree of fame among those who are
attracted by the occult and the mystic.

During these sessions of talking in his sleep Cayce would
often ramble on about nonmedical subjects as well. One of
his favorite subjects was Atlantis. In December 1943, Cayce
predicted that Atlantis would rise again. He set no exact
date for the great event, and since he always made his prophecies in obscure language it is difficult for anyone to figure
out what he meant. The key phrase is ". . . in Atlantis in
the period of the first upheavals and destruction that came
to the land, as must in the next generation come to other
land."

Cayce followers have interpreted this statement to mean
that the destructive upheavals associated with the rising of
the lost Atlantic continent will take place within the generation following the time the prediction was made. A generation
is thirty-three years, therefore the destruction seems to be
predicted to take place before the end of 1976.

The details of the coming disaster may be glimpsed in
other Cayce predictions:

"The greater portion of Japan must go into the sea."

"The greater change, as we will find, in America, will be
the North Atlantic Seaboard. Watch New York! . . . Portions
of the now east coast of New York, or New York City itself,
will in the main disappear. . . ."

One of the reasons that Cayce chose Virginia Beach as
a headquarters was that he believed that during the time of
the cataclysm it would be one of the few safe places in the
United States.

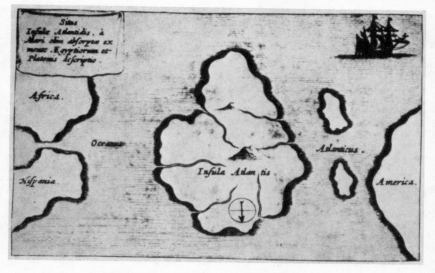

A map showing Atlantis that appeared in a book by Athanasius Kircher printed in 1678.

Cayce did not quite predict the final end of the world, but by the magnitude of the disasters he did predict he was coming pretty close.

In his mass of confusing and often contradictory predictions concerning the rising of Atlantis and the sinking of much of the rest of the world Cayce gives some other dates:

"Poseidia will be among the first portions of Atlantis to rise again—expect it in '68 and '69—not so far away." It was this part of the Cayce prediction that contributed mightily to a doomsday scare that gripped California in 1968 and 1969. (See Chapter 8.)

Cayce also seemed to indicate that Atlantis would rise somewhere near the Bahama Islands in the Caribbean. This sounds like an odd place for the island that was supposed to be just the other side of the Straits of Gibraltar. Yet considering where others have located Atlantis, the Bahamas is not the oddest place.

There have been persistent rumors that a great sunken city has been found by skin divers off the Bahamas, or that part of the sunken continent has already appeared above the waves, just as Edgar Cayce said it would. All of these reports are simply untrue. The area off the Bahamas has been explored many times by competent scientists. They have found no evidence that there ever was in that region any continental land mass or large "lost" island or anything else that could be remotely related to Atlantis.

Cayce died in obscurity in 1945. But since that time his fame has grown. In 1967 he was the subject of a best-selling biography. Scores of paperback books about him and his predictions have flooded the market. A popular mystic organization called the Association for Research and Enlightenment has been founded by the Cayce children to spread their father's teaching. Given the current interest in everything occult, Cayce's apocalyptic predictions will undoubtedly continue to feed end of the world fears for years to come.

There is yet another way in which man's thinking about earth's past has influenced his thoughts about earth's future. People who believe that the earth has been around for a long time worry less about it ending suddenly. An earth that is billions of years old seems stable, almost eternal. But if earth is comparatively young, say only a few thousand years old then it is easier to envision its imminent destruction.

The Manusmitri, a sacred book of the Hindus, placed the existence of the earth past, present, and future at 4.32 billion years. This was one "day" in the life of Brahma. The figure is a striking one since scientists now place the age of the earth at approximately 4.5 billion years. This correlation is not quite as impressive as it first appears, however, for the 4.32 billion years of the Hindu belief is to be the total age of the earth. At present the earth is supposed to be going through the seventh of fourteen great cycles of Brahma's "day." Thus by this reckoning the current age of the earth is only two billion years. But still two billion years is a long time and the Hindus are not notably beset by end-of-the-world fears.

The Western world has traditionally viewed the earth as fairly young. In 1650 Archbishop James Ussher of Ireland collected all of the age references in the Old Testament. From them he calculated that the earth had been created in the year 4004 B.C. This date appeared in the margin of the first chapter of Genesis in many printed copies of the Bible. Some scholars refined Ussher's date even further by stating that Creation began at nine in the morning of October 24, 4004 B.C.

In 1750 the French natural scientist the Comte de Buffon tried to calculate the age of the earth scientifically. He had a number of solid spheres made, all of them of the same size but of different materials—iron, copper, brass, limestone, and so forth. He then took the spheres to a blacksmith's shop and had them all heated to a red-hot temperature. Then he carefully recorded the time it took for the spheres to cool to the point where he could touch them with his bare hands without feeling the sensation of heat. After he gathered this information he made some elaborate calculations taking into account the actual size and composition of the earth. He came out with the figure that the time which had elapsed from the red-hot state of the primordial earth to the origin of life had been 74,832 years.

That at least was what Buffon said publicly. Privately he thought that the age of the earth probably would have to be reckoned in the millions, rather than the thousands of years. In one of his manuscripts he confessed, "When I counted only 74,000 or 75,000 years for the time passed since the formation of the planets, I gave notice that I constrained myself in order to oppose received ideas as little as possible." The idea that the earth was millions of years old would have scandalized Church authorities. Buffon already had had some mild problems with ecclesiastical officials and he wanted no more of them.

From Buffon's time to the present day the estimated age of the earth has been pushed back farther and farther. The current estimate of 4.5 billion years is about twice as long as the estimate that was held just twenty or thirty years ago by most scientists.

The world therefore has been around for a long time, and it has withstood a great deal during its long existence. The world has repeatedly failed to end as predicted. Yet our planet is not eternal, and one day the world will indeed come to an end. In the chapters that follow we will look at the ways in which this might really happen.

CHAPTER 4

The Comets: Omens and Menaces

God protect us from the Comet
And the Fury of the Norsemen
—MEDIEVAL PRAYER

Probably no astronomical event has set off more end-of-the-world panics and created more general consternation and confusion than the sudden appearance of a great comet in the heavens. You may recall that it was the appearance of a bright comet at the beginning of the year 1843 that helped to swell the ranks of William Miller's apocalyptic movement.

The well-publicized appearance of the most famous of all comets, Halley's comet, in 1910 inspired a whole rash of wild predictions. The comet, it was said, was going to collide with the earth and perhaps smash our puny planet to bits. In vain did astronomers point out that the orbit of Halley's comet was well-known, and had been for nearly two centuries. The head of the comet, its only solid part, would not come within many millions of miles of the earth, said the astronomers.

There was, however, a real possibility that the earth would pass through the gaseous tail of the comet (in fact it did). Some people got the head and the tail of the comet confused, while others were convinced that the tail of the comet contained poisonous gases. One enterprising Englishman took to selling comet pills—a harmless mixture of aspirin and sugar—to protect others from the effects of the poisonous gases.

The world wasn't smashed to bits, nobody was poisoned, in fact Halley's comet was a big disappointment in 1910. The science writer Clifford D. Simak—who was six years old at the time—was one of the millions who awaited the arrival of the famed comet.

"So our family walked out into a field and looked up in the sky, and there the comet was. It was a wispy thing and quite unspectacular and I was disappointed. For I had seen drawings in the newspapers which had represented it as a streak of fire from horizon to horizon.

"Halley's Comet, to tell you the solemn truth, was no great shakes back in 1910; but apparently there had been other years when it was worth the looking.

"And even wispy as it was, we were lucky people, for of all the millions who searched the heavens for it, there were few that year who saw Halley's Comet."

Halley's comet's next scheduled appearance is in about 1986. This time it may be as faint or fainter than it was in 1910, for Halley's comet is dying, and besides the brightness of comets is not reliable. There is at least an outside chance that the comet will not appear at all. But it is absolutely safe to predict that the mere expectation of the comet will inspire yet another rash of end-of-the-world scares, just as it has been doing for hundreds of years.

It is not surprising that comets have been invested with

Halley's comet. *Mount Wilson and Palomar Observatories*

awesome and terrible significance. A really bright comet can be one of the most impressive of celestial events. It looks like a huge fireball in the sky with a blazing tail trailing behind it. It just looks dangerous. A comet can be the brightest object in the night sky, outshining even the moon, and some comets have been so bright that they were visible in the daytime.

But in order to believe that a comet is of such a size, and such power that a collision with earth might literally tear this planet apart one must first know that the earth is not the largest object in the universe. Ancient man did not know this, and therefore was probably less frightened of comets than men have been in more recent times. Science writer Willy Ley speculated, "To primitive man comets were probably meaningless, just something luminous in the night sky."

Aristotle believed that all astronomical objects, the sun, moon, planets, and stars were regular and orderly. Comets seemed disorderly intruders. Therefore, Aristotle reasoned, comets could not be astronomical objects, but were rather some sort of disturbance in earth's atmosphere, caused by burning vapors from the ground. The implication was that comets were no mortal danger to the earth, though Aristotle did note, "When there are many comets . . . the years are clearly dry and windy." The winds, Aristotle thought were a by-product of the burning vapors.

The word "comet," by the way, has a rather benign origin considering the fear in which these objects came to be held. It comes from the Greek word *kometes* which means long-haired. The comet was often described as a "long-haired star" the picture being the "star" or head of the comet, with the long hair or tail trailing behind it.

Though Aristotle was dead wrong about the nature of comets he was attempting to explain them from a purely naturalistic point of view. Up until three hundred years ago very few had even attempted to explain comets as part of nature. Before Aristotle's time comets were beginning to be looked upon as objects of awe, even terror. Astrology had gotten a firm hold on the minds of most of the men of the world, including Aristotle's own Greeks. Attempting to divine the future by interpreting various natural events as signs, portents, or omens of things to come was an almost universal obsession.

To the astrologically minded the heavens were not so much a place of stars and planets, rather they were a gigantic book in which the gods or the fates or what have you had written out all of the future events in sign language. Everything that happened in the sky had some significance for earthly events. The only problem was figuring out rules for interpreting the signs.

In theory, astrology is an orderly practice, and comets do not really fit into the astrological scheme of things, any more than they did with Aristotle's view of the heavens. But since mankind has always been passionately interested in discovering what the future held for him, men have always rushed to interpret any unusual event in nature—the birth of a two-headed calf, a severe storm, a large flight of birds—as a signal that some major change was about to take place in human affairs. A comet is an unusual and often spectacular event in that great book of the heavens. It is easy to see how the appearance of a comet came to be invested with such awesome significance in the ancient world.

Though men believed that the appearance of a comet meant something big was about to happen it was not always agreed what this big event was to be. Usually the comet was interpreted as foretelling something that the interpreter greatly wished or feared.

In the year A.D. 69 a comet was visible over the city of Jerusalem. Jewish rebels held the city and were fighting a desperate battle against the Romans who were attempting to retake it. Jewish prophets urged the people of Jerusalem to climb to the roof of the temple where they could see the miraculous sign of their coming deliverance that God had provided for them. The Jewish prophets were wrong. The city was taken by the Romans the following year, and the temple, holiest of Jewish holy places, was burned.

Some Romans, on the other hand, interpreted the very same comet as an omen of doom for the Emperor Vitellius. As it turned out these Romans were quite right. Vitellius was one of Rome's least glorious emperors. He ruled for less than a year, and in the face of mounting opposition he tried to abdicate, but he was unable to escape the city. He was captured by the mob, led through the streets of Rome, and horribly executed.

The captured Jewish general Josephus, who switched to the Roman side after his capture, interpreted the comet as a sign of the triumph of the Roman general Vespasian. Vespasian had spearheaded the successful crushing of the Jewish revolt and had replaced the unfortunate Vitellius as emperor. He reigned successfully and reasonably well for ten years. Of course, Josephus made his "prediction" only after Vespasian, who was his friend and patron, was firmly in power, and so it was more than a little self-serving and not really a prediction at all.

As you can see, comets could mean all sorts of things. In the play *Julius Caesar* Shakespeare wrote:

When beggars die, there are not comets seen;
    The Heavens themselves blaze forth the death of princes.

On a much more mundane level, wine growers used to talk of a "comet year." This referred to the belief that the wine made in a year in which a great comet appeared would have a superior flavor.

Because of the enormous influence of Aristotle, comets were long regarded as "weather signs" that signified dry and windy weather.

Astrology remained influential and perfectly respectable in both Christian and Moslem lands throughout the Middle Ages. So comets remained signs of some important event, in the minds of most men. Usually they were considered signs of

God's wrath, rather than of his favor. Medieval Christians were generally more concerned with punishment, and gloomy, even apocalyptic, omens were much in favor. Here is a typical quote from a listing of comets: "Anno 1531, 1532 and 1533 comets were seen and at that time Satan hatched heretics."

However, a clever court astrologer would often interpret a comet as a sign of good fortune for the king or prince who employed him. Kings and princes were not well-disposed toward astrologers who predicted doom for *them*.

By the early sixteenth century there were a small number of men who started to wonder, not so much what the comets meant, but what they were. Modern astronomy really began in the sixteenth century, and just by chance that happened to be a particularly good time for the study of comets because a large number of bright comets were visible to the naked eye. Thus, though astronomers were already beginning to use the newly invented telescope, there were plenty of comets that could be seen even without them. And these comets naturally excited the interest and curiosity of the astronomers.

It is impossible to say how many large comets appear in an average century, because comets are too irregular, and our records of them are incomplete and do not go back far enough. It has been estimated that in every generation— that is, every thirty-three years—there is about one large comet visible to the naked eye. Yet in modern times there have been no really impressive comets seen since 1882. There have been comets, of course, plenty of them but they have either been pallid affairs like the 1910 appearance of Halley's comet or visible only with the aid of a telescope. There were nine large naked-eye comets recorded during the fifteenth century. People of the sixteenth century witnessed sixteen large naked-eye comets, and the seventeenth century saw another sixteen naked-eye comets. Small wonder that man's superstitious awe of comets rose to new heights during these centuries. But man's knowledge of comets also increased dramatically.

The turning point in the scientific study of comets came with the great comet of 1577. It was an enormously bright object and was observed by all the astronomers of the day. Observations from different parts of the world were collected by the great Danish astronomer Tycho Brahe. With all of these observations of the same object from distant points, Tycho was able to calculate that the comet had been "supra-lunar," that is, farther away from the earth than the moon. So Aristotle's old idea of comets being some sort of distur-bance in the earth's atmosphere was finally laid to rest.

Now if a comet that appeared as large as the comet of 1577 was in fact farther away than the moon, then the comet itself must be huge. Tycho calculated that the moon was about 225,000 miles from earth (actually it is about 238,857 miles away). The comet of 1577 he said was 9 million miles from earth. The head of this comet was over 1,200 miles in diameter and the tail over 300,000 miles long.

With such dimensions it is easy to see how comets were changed in the minds of many from omens of doom to agents of doom. There were those who continued to regard comets as signs rather than real dangers. The followers of William Miller saw the comet as an omen of Judgment Day rather than as the instrument God would use to put an end to the world. Yet even those who were no longer firm believers in signs and omens could not shake the idea that comets were somehow evil and dangerous. Many envisioned this huge fiery body rushing straight toward earth and perhaps smash-ing our planet to bits.

Could it happen? Could a collision with a large comet bring about the end of the world? In order to answer this question we must first know more about what a comet is, where comets come from, and where they go.

The nucleus of a comet has been likened to a "dirty iceberg." The ice in this case is not just frozen water (though some H_2O may be present), but it is mainly frozen gases like methane and ammonia. Embedded in these frozen gases, and perhaps surrounding them, are small solid particles, stones, or chunks of metal, ranging from the size of a grain of dust up to perhaps the size of a small pebble.

Like the planets, the comets travel around the sun. But their orbits are not nearly so regular, and they are usually much larger. A comet may travel from far beyond the orbit of Pluto, the farthest planet, till it comes quite close to the sun, then it makes a sharp turn and travels outward again. Not all comets have orbits that large, some seventy known comets go out only as far as Jupiter's orbit before beginning their return trip to the sun. These comets complete their orbit in from 5 to 10 years. Comet Encke has the shortest orbital period of any known comet, 3.3 years.

The fame of Halley's comet is due not so much to its size or brilliance, but to the fact that it was the first comet in history to be successfully predicted. In 1705 the British astronomer Edmund Halley published a paper which suggested that comets orbited the sun and that the same comets had been seen many different times in history. Halley computed the orbits of twenty-four comets that had been seen in the past. Since the orbits of comets are not completely regular, and since the observations at Halley's command were far from complete not everyone accepted his conclusion.

The computations that gave Halley a cometary namesake were those regarding the comets that had appeared in 1456, 1531, 1607, and 1682. All of these Halley said were really a single comet that had an orbital period of about seventy-five years. He predicted that the same comet would appear again in 1758 or 1759. With the information he had available Halley could not be more precise about the return of the comet. Even today with vastly more sophisticated instruments and a larger volume of observations than were available to Edmund Halley, astronomers still cannot be exact about comets, because cometary orbits tend to vary in unpredictable ways. Halley himself died in 1742, but as he had predicted the comet returned again. It was first spotted by telescope on Christmas night of 1758, and within a few months it was a blazing spectacle overhead. Halley's prediction was spectacularly confirmed and his theories about the orbits of comets established beyond a quibble.

The perihelion of Halley's comet, that is the point at which the comet is closest to the sun, is inside the orbit of the planet Mercury. At that point the comet is a mere 18 million miles from the surface of the sun. The aphelion of the comet, the point at which it is farthest from the sun, is out beyond the orbit of the planet Neptune.

While out on the fringes of the solar system comets remain solidly frozen. But as they approach the sun, the heat vaporizes some of the gas from the front of the comet. This vaporized gas is pushed by the solar wind (an outward streaming cloud of subatomic particles) away from the sun. It is this vaporized material that forms the tail of the comet. Because of the pressure of the solar wind the tail always points away from the sun. Traveling in toward the sun the tail trails behind the comet. Traveling outward away from the sun the tail trails ahead of the comet.

Though a comet does not completely "melt" on its close approach to the sun, it obviously does lose considerable material, and so comets cannot last forever. How long can they keep orbiting the sun? We really don't know. Halley's comet has been observed regularly since the year 163 B.C., and until its last appearance it was usually a pretty spectacular sight. (Ironically, Halley's comet blazed through the skies in the year 1066, the year that William the Conqueror invaded England, and one of the major turning points in English history. What an omen that must have seemed like!) But Halley's comet may be dying now; that is why we cannot be sure that it will ever appear again.

Other comets that had been observed regularly have simply disappeared, and astronomers assume that they have just melted away. In December of 1845 astronomers watched for the approach of the comet Biela. It appeared on schedule alright, but it had apparently split into two parts. In 1866 when the comet should have appeared again it did not. Comet Biela had "died." Scientists estimate that on the average comets do not "live" more than a few thousand years.

As the frozen gases, which make up the bulk of the comet's nucleus vaporize into space, they release some of the solid material that was trapped in it. These bits of solid material trail along behind the comet, and ultimately become strung out along its orbit. When the earth passes through the orbit of a comet it may encounter a mass of these particles. As the particles hit the atmosphere they burn up. This is the cause of the regular meteorite "showers." Though such "showers" can be impressive—hundreds or thousands of "shooting stars" might be observed every hour during an in- the earth's atmosphere and hits the ground. On the other hand, a good-sized meteorite will burn on its trip through the earth's atmosphere, but there will be enough of it left to strike the ground. The conclusion is that all of the solid particles associated with a comet are quite small.

You can see that for all their showiness comets don't have much mass. Scientists estimate that there is more ma-

Imaginative drawing of the appearance of Halley's Comet in 1910. *Courtesy of the American Museum of Natural History*

terial in a cubic inch of air at ground level than there is in two thousand cubic miles of a comet's tail. So we don't have to worry about a comet's tail, or passing through the orbit of a comet or anything like that.

But what about a direct head-on collision with a comet? How big and massive are the heads of comets? The head of a comet consists of two parts. The solid nucleus and the glowing, cloudlike coma. We only have to worry about the nucleus. Of course, comets vary a good deal in size. One estimate is that the nucleus of an average comet is 1.2 miles in diameter. But a really huge comet may have a nucleus thousands of miles in diameter. Any comet that hits the earth directly is going to pack quite a wallop.

How likely is such a collision? Not very. There are plenty of comets around (though no one knows how many) but considering the vastness of space the chance of earth and a comet being at the same place at the same time seems slight. One theory holds that if comets were spread evenly throughout the solar system, then there would be one about every 2.7 billion miles—which is the distance from earth to Neptune. Dr. Otto Struve, professor of astronomy at the University of California at Berkeley, has estimated that the likelihood of a direct collision between earth and a comet would occur only about once in every 200 million years. That is why it seems almost miraculous that the earth really did collide with a comet, not back in some dim period of prehistory, but in 1908, just two years before people all over the world were worrying needlessly about the earth colliding with Halley's comet. What makes the cometary collision of 1908 even more amazing is that at the time no one knew what had happened. Even today there is some dispute over whether the earth actually collided with a comet or with something else.

From the beginning the story of the 1908 collision was shrouded in mystery. At a meeting of British scientists in 1908 one meteorologist pointed out that his instruments showed that powerful air waves of unknown origin had passed across England from north to south on June 30, 1908. He could offer no explanation for his instrument readings. As it turned out practically every weather station in the world with sensitive barometric equipment registered similar readings.

On that same date, in Russia and Germany, seismographs, the machines used for measuring earthquakes, recorded a mild shock. The earth tremor seemed to be centered in Siberia in the vicinity of the small town of Kansk, a region in which earthquakes were virtually unknown.

On the night of June 30, 1908, witnesses in Aberdeen, Scotland, testified that as the sun set the sky grew darker and then suddenly lighter again—"almost as bright as daylight." A similar phenomenon was observed in other parts of the country. There was nothing that could account for the strange light.

For the next few days the people of northern Scotland witnessed sunsets of unusual brilliance and spectacular color.

It took a long time for scientists to establish any connection between these different odd phenonena. In fact it was not until 1920 that the story of what happened on June 30, 1908, really began to unfold. At that time what seemed like wild and fantastic rumors began to filter out of an extremely remote area in the midst of the taiga forests of Siberia. The rumors told of a gigantic explosion that had taken place sometime during the summer of 1908. Then the other information about the strange barometric readings, the earth tremors, and odd lights and sunsets were recalled.

The problem of what had happened on June 30, 1908,

Cartoon showing people in Central Park preparing for the arrival of Halley's Comet in 1910. *Courtesy of the American Museum of Natural History*

over central Siberia was of particular interest to a young Russian scientist named Leonid Kulik. Quite by accident Kulik had run across a calendar printed in Siberia. On the back of the sheets were local stories, and one of these stories told of the "piece of the sun" that had fallen into the taiga forest.

In 1920 Russia was exhausted by revolution and war but Kulik managed to get enough money from the authorities for himself and two associates to travel to Siberia in 1921. He reached Kansk and found many people who remembered the 1908 event vividly. But he also discovered that the explosion itself had taken place considerably to the north of Kansk, in the middle of the dense forest. The area was virtually inaccessible. This northern forest is bitterly cold during the winter. When the snow melts, during the brief Siberian summer, the whole region is turned into insect-infested marshlands. The area was thinly populated by primitive Tunguska tribesmen, who lived mainly by herding reindeer. Kulik had to return to Leningrad before he had any chance to locate the

La comète.

Imagined effects of the comet of 1811. Among the things supposedly produced by the comet were volcanic eruptions and good wine. *Courtesy of the American Museum of Natural History*

impact site. It was not until 1927 that he was able to return to Siberia.

In March of 1927 an expedition set out to find the spot where something had hit the earth in 1908. Most of the trip was carried out on a raft that was laboriously poled along the small rivers that cut through the marshland. In three months the expedition was able to cover just a little over forty miles—but they found the spot. It was in a swampy basin near the Podkamennaya (Stony) Tunguska river.

After his investigations Kulik wrote up a report on the "Podkamennaya Tunguska impact." Kulik was not trying to be sensational, but the report made sensational reading anyway. A circle of trees from twenty to twenty-five miles in diameter had been uprooted by the shock of the impact. The Russians have estimated that as many as 80 million trees were felled. All of the trees in the circle of destruction point outward from the impact site. All of the uprooted trees were badly charred, and trees still standing around the perimeter of the circle showed signs of having had their tops burned off. The charred bodies of thousands of reindeer had been found after the explosion.

The people of the region were very superstitious, and at first they didn't want to talk about the event for fear that it would bring bad luck. But finally they did talk. One of the witnesses to the cataclysm had been at the trading post of Vanavara some forty miles from the impact center.

"There was a fiery flame in the northwest, which gave off such heat that my shirt nearly caught fire. I felt as if I were enveloped in flame. I noticed that this miracle covered a space of [a little over a mile]. . . . I only had time to note the extent and the flame disappeared. After the flame disappeared there was an explosion which threw me off my feet a distance of seven feet or more . . . The glass and frames of

Medieval representation of Halley's comet as it appeared over England in 1066. That was the year in which the Battle of Hastings, one of the pivotal battles of English history was fought. *Yerkes Observatory*

my house broke and clods of earth were spit up from the square in front of my hut."

At Kansk some three hundred miles from the impact center a man recalled ". . . one sharp thud, then dull noises like an underground roaring. The thud was so severe that one of the workmen fell into the water."

Witnesses had seen a huge fireball, exceeding the sun in brilliance, flash across the sky. This had been followed by the noises and the shock waves. After the impact witnesses described seeing a "pillar of fire" about a mile across and rising to an estimated height of twelve miles. This "pillar of fire" Kulik believed was caused by the almost instantaneous com-

bustion of millions of trees over a four-hundred-square-mile
area.

It was now obvious that this tremendous impact had
caused the other phenomena that puzzled scientists in 1908.
Both the barometric and seismographic disturbances had resulted directly from the force of the impact. The lengthening
of the hours of daylight and the brilliant sunsets were caused
by a huge cloud of dust that was flung high into the air. A

The comet of 1527. *New York Public Library Picture Collection*

large dust cloud high in the atmosphere catches the sun's rays and reflects them downward for a time, even after the sun itself has sunk below the horizon. Ash clouds from major volcanic explosions have also produced brilliant sunsets throughout the world.

Kulik and practically every scientist who read his report first assumed that the earth had been struck by a large meteorite. But if a meteorite had indeed been the cause where was the impact crater? Kulik found that some of the rocks in the center of the area of destruction seemed to have been "folded into small wrinkles." But there was no big crater of the type customarily dug by large meteorites. There were repeated expeditions to the area, and it was minutely photographed from the air. But still not a trace of a crater has been found.

Scientists then assumed that the meteorite had somehow exploded shortly before impact and that only comparatively small meteorite fragments reached the earth and thus created no large crater. But if this were true what happened to the fragments? Nearly a half-century of digging had turned up just a few ounces of meteoric material from the impact area. Since meteorites fall all over the earth all of the time, if you sift through the soil at any randomly chosen spot you might find almost as much meteoric material as was found in the Tunguska impact area.

It seemed as though the earth had been struck by a huge meteorite which had vaporized upon impact. And there lay the solution to the mystery. You recall we described comets as "dirty icebergs." They are just the sort of bodies that would vaporize upon impact. The gases would either burn up or mix with the atmosphere, and within an hour there would be no trace of the body which had caused the catastrophe. The bits of meteoric material found in the area may have originally been part of the comet.

The Russian Academy of Science endorsed the comet hypothesis in 1957. Some astronomers even believed that they could identify the comet. The comet Pons-Winnecke would have been in the vicinity of the earth on June 30, 1908. However, that comet had been seen several times since 1908, so the whole comet could not have been the culprit. But if comet Pons-Winnecke had split, like comet Biela had been observed to do, a small portion of that comet might have hit the earth. The identification of comet Pons-Winnecke has not satisfied all astronomers. Indeed, even the comet idea has not been universally accepted. There are still a lot of wild stories that circulate about the "Podkamennaya Tunguska impact."

In 1960 a group of Russian scientific amateurs visited the Tunguska area and came back with a story that the region was highly radioactive. This story was reported by the official Soviet press and picked up by newspapers all over the world. Soon the theory was advanced that the Podkamennaya Tunguska impact had not been caused by a meteorite or comet at all, but by the explosion of a nuclear-powered spaceship from another planet. This story was nonsense. There never was any unusual radiation at the Tunguska site, but one still hears the spaceship theory repeated from time to time.

A theory very nearly as startling as the one about the spaceship has been advanced by Lincoln LaPaz, director of the Institute of Meteoritics at the University of New Mexico, and one of the world's leading experts on meteorites. It almost seems as if Dr. LaPaz is unwilling to assign the responsibility for the Podkamennaya Tunguska impact to anything but his beloved meteorites. He suggests that this particular meteorite was made up of antimatter, or contraterrene matter, as it is sometimes called.

Dr. LaPaz writes, "What would happen now if a contraterrene meteorite penetrated into the ordinary matter of earth? The answer is that just as an electron and a positron mutually annihilate each other when they collide, so the meteorite and an equal mass of the earth target itself would vanish at the instant of impact."

The result would be a natural nuclear explosion of vast power. Dr. LaPaz continues, "Such an explosion would account for all the sensational phenomena observed at the time of the Podkamennaya Tunguska incident; and, furthermore, would explain why the Russian investigators have never succeeded in recovering meteorites from this fall."

Despite Dr. LaPaz's ingenious theory, the majority of scientists believe that a comet was responsible for the Tunguska incident.

How big was the comet that struck Siberia? Russian scientists have estimated that it was several miles in diameter and weighed close to a million tons.

One astronomer who was calculating the path of the comet that struck Siberia noted that its impact was at exactly the same latitude as the city of Leningrad (in 1908 the city was called St. Petersburg and was the capital of the Russian empire). If the comet had been just a few hours earlier in its orbit it would have hit the city and reduced it to rubble, probably killing every inhabitant.

If such a collision occurred today, it might well trigger a nuclear war before anyone had a chance to figure out what had really happened.

The comet that struck the Tunguska area in 1908 was a fairly small one. If one of the really large comets impacted with earth the effects could be cataclysmic. If Professor Struve's calculations are correct, the odds are heavily against another cometary collision with earth for about another 200 million years.

Figuring the odds on comets, however, is an uncertain business at best, because no one really knows how many comets there are, where they come from, or what sets them

Site of the Podkamennaya Tunguska impact. Though this photo was taken some twenty years after the impact the destruction was still very evident. *Sovfoto*

traveling toward the sun. The best guess today is that comets are part of the debris left over when the solar system was formed out of a cosmic cloud of gas and dust. A vast hollow spherical "cloud" containing as many as 100 million comets is believed to hover on the far fringes of the solar system, millions upon millions of miles beyond the orbit of Pluto. Recently astronomers have postulated the existence of an inner comet belt as well. But even 100 million comets would only have one-tenth of the total mass of the earth.

The comets of this cloud are in orbit around the sun but they remain so far out that they never come within the vicinity of the earth. In fact, the comets of this cloud are entirely theoretical for they cannot be detected by even the most sensitive of today's astronomical instruments. But every once in a while something disturbs a comet in this "cloud"; it may be a collision with another comet or the gravitational field of a passing star. Whatever it is the disturbance causes this comet to begin its long trip toward the sun, and just incidentally into the vicinity of our earth.

The exceptionally high number of bright comets seen during the fifteenth and sixteenth centuries may have been caused by some sort of major disturbance in the cometary cloud. So there always exists the possibility that there will be a sudden and dramatic increase in the number of comets in the vicinity of the earth, and thus the chance of collision with a comet would go up.

But on balance, we may happily conclude that we really don't have to worry much about comets ever bringing an end to the world or that a cometary collision will be the source of a major disaster that will take a large number of human lives.

One final note on comets. Those people who are addicted to propounding cataclysmic theories about the earth are also frequently addicted to comets as well. Back in 1696 the

Reverend William Whiston of England advanced some theories about how the close approach of certain comets throughout history had profound effects upon the earth. A comet, he said, had caused the biblical flood. Now Reverend Whiston was a respected mathematician, in fact, he succeeded Isaac Newton as professor of mathematics at Cambridge. His book *The Cause of the Deluge Demonstrated* (London, 1711) was very influential. Whiston formed his theories before Halley had discovered that comets regularly orbit the sun. But still such ideas about comets and catastrophes were scientifically and historically untenable, even in his own day, and he seems to have been more influenced by the comet's evil reputation than by anything he had been able to calculate about them.

The next great comet-cataclysm theorist was Ignatius Donnelly. His *Ragnarök* proposed that all manner of worldwide upheavals had been caused by the close approach of large comets.

The twentieth century's leading cataclysmic scholar, Dr. Immanuel Velikovsky, has theorized that thirty-five hundred years ago a huge chunk of material erupted out of the planet Jupiter, streaked past earth causing all sorts of cataclysmic interruptions in the normal functions of this planet, and finally the piece of Jupiter settled down in orbit around the sun, where it came to be called the planet Venus. It would be pointless to try to argue about Dr. Velikovsky's theories here. Suffice it to say that not a single reputable scientist anywhere has agreed with him. The point is that this mythical castoff from the planet Jupiter might have been called a planetary fragment, a protoplanet, a meteorite, a planetoid, an asteroid, or something like that, but Velikovsky chose to call it a comet.

The powerful reputation of the comet lingers to this day.

CHAPTER 5

Meteorites: Bombs from Heaven

A meteor is the flash of light
Made by a falling meteorite
As it rushes through the air in flight—
I hope to gosh this answer's right!
—ANONYMOUS

Before we get into the substance of this chapter we had better clear up some terminology. Otherwise the subject can become rather confusing. The meteorite expert Lincoln La-Paz is fond of quoting the little bit of doggerel poetry above, that was written by an unnamed freshman astronomy student.

The answer is right, though in ordinary speech and writing the words "meteor" and "meteorite" are often used interchangeably. A meteor is the light streak or "shooting star" that we see in the sky. A meteorite is the solid object that caused the streak. To be exact, a meteorite is what remains of the solid object after it has hit the earth. While this body is still out in space, it is correctly referred to as a *meteoroid*.

A really big meteoroid is also called an *asteroid*, or sometimes a *planetoid*.

Most of this terminology is simply inappropriate today and reflects ancient beliefs rather than modern knowledge. "Meteor" comes from a Greek word meaning "a thing of the air." That is why the study of weather is called meteorology —it has nothing to do with the meteorites. Meteorites themselves are certainly not things of the air, they are rocks and chunks of metal from outer space. But the words have been in use too long now to be changed.

Meteorites regularly strike the earth, and really big meteorites have gouged out enormous craters on our planet's surface. Yet oddly enough people didn't worry much about meteorites bringing an end to the world; in fact, for quite a while the most advanced scientific thinkers in the world did not believe that stones could fall from the sky at all.

In ancient times, however, people knew perfectly well that stones fell from the sky. The earliest known record of a meteorite is found in the treasure list of a Hittite king compiled in the sixteenth century B.C. There is a reference to "black iron of heaven from the sky." The Roman writer Livy mentions a shower of stones that were supposed to have fallen in Rome around the year 654 B.C. Chinese records speak of a large meteorite which struck several chariots and killed ten men in 616 B.C.

The fall of a large meteorite was often considered such a special event that kings or other rulers in the vicinity of the fall would mint special coins or medals known as *betyls,* in honor of the event. The Greek historian and traveler Herodotus actually saw one of the meteorites honored by a betyl, and he described it as: "A large stone, which on the lower side is round, and above runs gradually to a point. It has nearly the form of a cone, and is of a black color. People say of it in earnest that it fell from Heaven."

Meteorites were not merely honored, they were often worshiped. A meteorite is almost certainly mentioned in the Bible; in Acts 19:35 the town clerk of Ephesus cries: "Men of Ephesus, what man is there who does not know that the city of Ephesians is temple keeper of the great Artemis, and of the sacred stone that fell from the sky?" (Revised Standard Version translation)

A meteorite has been found in an Aztec temple, and meteorites have been interred in Indian burial mounds in North America. The Black Stone of the Kaaba, in Mecca, which is the most sacred object in all Islam is probably a meteorite. No one is really sure, however, for the stone is so sacred that no scientist has ever been allowed to study it, and non-Moslems are not even allowed to approach it. The stone was worshipped long before the Moslem religion came into being and was so holy that the pagans would not abandon it after their conversion to Islam, so they incorporated it into the new faith.

Once a scientist was actually able to observe a meteorite become an object of worship. On December 2, 1880, a six-pound meteorite fell to earth in a field near Andhara, India. A scientist quickly arrived on the spot to investigate the fall. By the time he got there he found that the meteorite had been picked up, cleaned and put in the charge of two Brahman priests who were busily collecting money to build a temple in which the holy object could be displayed.

The scientist was not allowed to touch the object, but he did get a good look at it and was able to identify it as a typical meteorite. Crowds of worshipers were flocking to the unfinished temple with offerings of flowers, food, and money. The stone had been named Adbhuta-Nath, "the miraculous god."

Since the fall of meteorites, or meteor showers, were strange and apparently unnatural events, they were regarded as omens of either ill or good fortune. A quote from Shakespeae's *Richard II* expresses a typical attitude:

The bay-trees in our country are all wither'd
And meteors fright the fixed stars of heaven;
The pale-faced moon looks bloody on the earth
And lean-look'd prophets whisper fearful change, . . .

These signs forerun the death or fall of kings.

On the other hand, a meteorite might be regarded as a sign of good luck or divine favor. On November 16, 1492, a meteorite weighing nearly three hundred pounds fell in Alsace, near the battle lines separating the armies of the Holy Roman Empire and France. The Emperor Maximilian had the stone carried to his castle. He called his councilors together to help him determine what the fall of the stone meant. The council declared that the meteorite was a sign of God's favor. The emperor had the stone hung in the parish church in Ensisheim. We cannot be sure if he really regarded the meteorite as a sign of divine favor, or whether saying that it was amounted to a clever propaganda move. But the Ensisheim stone became the first meteorite of witnessed fall to be preserved.

You can see that for ages people had correctly regarded meteorites as stones that fell from the sky. Therefore, it is very strange that in the eighteenth century, a century of great scientific progress, many scientists doubted this fact. They said that there was no "proof" that meteorites came from the sky and rejected the thousands of eyewitness accounts as fables and relics from an age of superstition. The scientists of the influential French Academy were particularly scornful of the idea that meteorites fell from the sky, and it was a brave scientist indeed who dared to openly oppose the opinion of the formidable Academy.

Two Yale University professors announced that over three hundred pounds of meteorites had fallen in Weston, Connecticut, in December 1807. This announcement was supposed to have prompted Thomas Jefferson to say, "I could more easily believe that two Yankee professors lie, than that stones would fall from heaven." Jefferson was no pigheaded fool, he was deeply interested in science and very knowledgeable about it. He was simply expressing the opinion held by most of the educated men of his day.

A few scientists examined meteorites from different parts of the world and finding that they all showed signs of having been burnt or fused in their trip through the atmosphere, stubbornly insisted that they had indeed fallen from the sky. The controversy became more and more heated. At the end of the eighteenth century there were a number of well-observed and quite spectacular meteorite falls. Ultimately resistance to the idea that meteorites came from beyond the earth's atmosphere crumbled.

The eighteenth-century scientific attitude toward meteorites does not represent one of the more glorious chapters in the history of science. Many people who hold unorthodox views on scientific subjects point to "stones from the sky" controversy just to prove that the scientific "establishment" can be as dogmatic as anyone else.

The followers of William Miller had regarded the meteor shower of 1833 as yet another sign that the world was about to end. But in general meteorites were not looked upon as either signs or agents of the end of the world. Certainly they never inspired the epidemics of superstitious terror that comets had long inspired. Ironically, meteorites are much more dangerous to earth than are comets.

Comets are comparatively rare, but the earth is under

continuous bombardment from meteorites. Harvard Observatory has estimated that some 100 *billion* meteoroids hit the earth's atmosphere every twenty-four hours. Of these, only a tiny percentage ever reach the earth's surface as meteorites. Estimated daily averages for meteorites striking earth range from one to thirty.

Most of these meteorites are fairly small and have done little damage. Occasionally small meteorites have fallen through roofs and broken windows. In 1954 a meteorite crashed through the roof of a house in Sylacauga, Alabama, bounced off a radio and hit a woman on the leg. All the falls of large meteorites so far have been in uninhabited areas. Except for one dubious ancient Chinese record, no one has ever been known to have been killed by a falling meteorite.

The largest known meteorite to fall in recent times struck the Ussuri valley of eastern Siberia on February 12, 1947. The region was dense and inhospitable in a forest, similar to the Tunguska area that had been hit, probably by a comet, in 1908. The meteorite impact broke windows and shook crockery in a nearby village, but no one was hurt. By a remarkable coincidence an artist in the village happened to be making sketches as he saw the huge fireball streak through the sky. He made a painting of the scene before the memory could fade from his mind. Reproductions of this painting are in scientific museums all around the world and it was even put on a Russian postage stamp.

The Ussuri meteorite broke up shortly before hitting the earth, so the impact did not create one big crater, but a whole area of smaller ones. These range in size from little bowl-like craters to one twenty-eight yards across and six yards deep. This crater is large enough to hold a two-story house.

Trees over a wide area were uprooted and broken into

This large meteorite from Oregon is now on display at the American Museum of Natural History in New York City.
Courtesy of the American Museum of Natural History

pieces. Huge trees had been thrown forty or fifty yards by the force of the impact. Fist-sized chunks of meteoric material were found embedded in some tree trunks. One Soviet investigator compared the scene to a bombed-out area.

Ultimately some twenty thousand meteoric fragments from the size of a grain of sand to a chunk weighing 3,839 pounds were recovered from the Ussuri impact area. The total weight of the recovered fragments was approximately twenty-three tons. At least twice that amount is believed to still be scattered about the crater field.

The meteorite that struck at Ussuri was a lightweight compared to some of the meteorites that have hit the earth in the past. How big was the biggest meteorite ever found? We don't really know for it was lost almost immediately after it was found. The story is a strange one.

In 1916 a captain in the Mauritanian army was taken by a native guide to a meteorite buried in the dunes of the Adrar desert in the western part of the Sahara. The visit was made at night, and the guide was very secretive and very nervous. What the captain could see was a mass of material measuring an estimated 300 feet by 120 feet, though the largest part of it seemed still buried in the sand. The captain made no map or notes on the location of the mass, but he did bring back a small ten-pound fragment he found lying on the top of it. This fragment proved to be a genuine meteorite.

When scientists later tried to locate the main body of this mass of meteoric material they confronted a wall of silence. The original guide had died, apparently poisoned, and all of the other natives consistently denied knowledge of the Adrar mass, though they certainly must have known where it was.

The largest generally recognized meteorite crater in the world is in the Arizona desert near Winslow. It has been variously called Meteor Crater (a name that annoys all purists of meteoritic terminology), Barringer Crater, or Arizona Crater. Whatever you want to call it, it is everybody's idea of what a meteorite crater should look like.

Meteor Crater is an almost perfect circle, four-fifths of a mile across, with a circumference of nearly three miles. All around the rim of the crater is a sort of wall 130 to 160 feet high. The material for this "wall" was forced up by the enormous pressure of the meteorite when it struck. From the edge of this wall the inside of the crater drops sharply to a depth of 550 feet. You could put the Washington Monument in the middle of Meteor Crater, and only six feet of

Meteor Crater, Arizona was probably formed by the explosive force released by the impact of a large meteorite, or cluster of meteorites. *U.S. Department of the Interior, Geological Survey*

it would stick up over the rim. What is more the crater was once deeper, but the action of the weather has filled it in somewhat. The impact pulverized and blew out some 300 million tons of rock.

How big of a meteorite dug this enormous crater? We don't really know. Fragments of meteoric material have been found scattered over a wide area. For nearly twenty years expensive drilling operations were carried on at the bottom of the crater in an attempt to locate the main mass of the meteorite which was assumed to be buried deep in the ground. No main mass was ever found. Now it is generally believed either that the heat developed by the meteorite as it plummeted through the atmosphere caused it to break up on impact or that the object that struck earth was not a single meteorite but a mass of smaller meteorites all packed together. Estimates of total size and weight vary widely. One expert estimated that the crater was created when an object some five hundred feet in diameter and weighing about 10 million tons struck the earth. But another and later estimate was that the crater could have been formed by a meteorite just eighty feet in diameter and weighing only sixty-three thousand tons.

In his book *The Elements Rage,* Frank W. Lane imagined this scene of the descent and impact of the meteoroid that took place in what is now Arizona some ten to fifty thousand years ago. "Friction with the air makes the surface incandescent as the oxygen in the atmosphere blowtorches the iron. From this great flying mass, sputtering chunks large as houses, fly off as the meteoroid, traveling at a low angle, nears the ground. A huge cylinder of superheated air is forced along by the meteoroid and, as it strikes, this air is forced across the surrounding countryside in a fiery blast that instantaneously scorches every living thing for a hundred miles in every direction.

"When the meteorite strikes, the whole earth is jolted. The meteorite tears its way through a quarter of a mile of solid rock. A wall of flame shoots 20 miles high and the thunder of the colossal impact goes round the world."

There is no reason to believe that the meteorite that blasted out the crater in Arizona was the largest ever to hit the earth. It almost certainly was not. You recall that we said that this crater was the largest generally accepted meteorite crater on earth. But there are some other scars on the earth's surface that may have been caused by the impact of much larger meteorites. The largest of these suspected craters is the Vredefort Ring in South Africa which is some thirty miles wide.

The problem in recognizing any ancient meteorite craters on the earth is that erosion and various sorts of geologic activity like mountain building tend to wear away or otherwise obscure the characteristic features of an impact crater. To confuse matters still more, there are various geophysical processes which can create features that look like impact craters but are not. For example, in the subarctic region of Quebec Canada there is a hole in the earth some 2 miles across and 800 feet deep with a circumference of 6.8 miles. It was once regarded as the largest meteorite crater on earth. But recent investigations of the area have thrown serious doubt on the idea that this New Quebec Crater or Chubb Crater is really a meteorite crater after all. On the other hand, up until the 1920s there were many scientists who did not believe that the Arizona crater had been blasted out by a meteorite. Rather they attributed it to natural earthly processes. The debate over what is and what is not a crater is likely to continue for a long time.

If erosion and geologic activity were not continually obliterating ancient features of the earth's surface, the face of this planet might more closely resemble the ravaged and

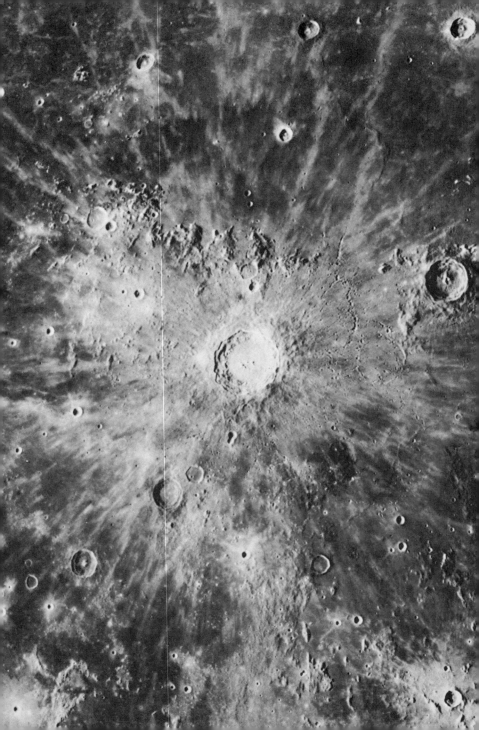

pockmarked surface of the moon. With no atmosphere and little or no geologic activity a crater on the moon will remain distinct and identifiable millions of years after it was formed and long after it would have been obliterated on the earth.

Do the number of large craters on the moon give us an accurate picture of the number of large meteorites that might have hit the earth through the ages? Well perhaps, but we are not sure that all of the large craters on the moon were caused by meteoric impact. Some of them certainly were, but some, perhaps the largest of them, were caused by some sort of volcanic activity. Moon exploration will ultimately settle the dispute between those scientists who ascribe most of the craters to meteorites and those who favor the volcanic theory. It may be significant, however, that the Mariner spacecraft pictures of the planet Mars indicate that its face also has numerous craters.

Amid all the controversy, this much we can be certain of; large meteorites have struck the earth in the past, causing considerable damage, and large meteorites will continue to strike the earth from time to time in the future as long as the earth exists.

Are there meteorites out in space that are large enough to cause a worldwide cataclysm if they struck earth? And if so, do such objects regularly enter the vicinity of the earth? The answer to both of these questions unfortunately is yes. The objects are the "male" asteroids.

The mere existence of the asteroids is, in fact, a little disturbing. Astronomical calculations indicate that there should be a planet orbiting between Mars and Jupiter. But it isn't there. Instead there is a belt of cosmic debris—chunks of rocks and metals orbiting the sun. These range in size from an asteroid named Ceres that is some 480 miles in diameter and Pallas 300 miles in diameter to millions of

'he crater Copernicus on the moon is considered a typical
ınar impact crater. *Mount Wilson and Palomar Observatories*

chunks the size of basketballs, to billions of smaller fragments. The asteroid belt is not a solid mass of debris. The
material is thinly spread through space. A spaceship passing
through the belt would encounter an asteroid only by chance.
But there is enough material out there for astronomers to
realize that something happened or failed to happen in that
segment of the solar system.

There are two principal theories regarding the asteroid
belt. The first is that the asteroids are the remains of a planet
that at one time or another broke up. Just how this planet
might have broken up is unknown. The planet could have
been shattered by a head-on collision with another body of
about the same mass or it might have exploded from a
buildup of heat and pressure due to natural radioactivity.
Inevitably it has been proposed that this planet was blown
apart during a thermonuclear war among its inhabitants, but
this theory belongs more in the realm of science fiction. A
combination of explosion and collision might have done the
job. First the planet exploded into large fragments due to
natural radioactivity, then repeated collision between these
fragments produced the asteroid belt as we know it today.
But not all scientists find these explanations satisfactory.

Still even the possibility that a planet in the solar system was broken up by an unknown catastrophe should make
us a little uncomfortable about the safety of our own planet.
If it happened once, it could happen again.

A more recent theory contends that the asteroid belt
never was a planet, but that it is the makings of a planet
that somehow failed to be born. The most widely accepted
theory about the formation of the solar system is that the
sun and the planets condensed out of a cloud of cosmic gas
and dust. A planet should have formed between Mars and
Jupiter, but it didn't—the original dust and some large
chunks are still there, however.

Of the two theories, the one which holds that the asteroids are the remains of a shattered planet is probably the most widely accepted. But the asteroid belt does not merely serve as a warning that a planet might be destroyed; the asteroids themselves can present a real danger to the earth.

The large asteroids that remain in their orbital path between Mars and Jupiter are of course no danger to us. These large asteroids have been given feminine names, and since there are so many of them, astronomers have gotten pretty hard up for names. There are asteroids named Photographia, Limburgia, Gesha, and even Rockefellia. Astronomers no longer even try to discover new asteroids in the belt.

A few large asteroids have broken out of the belt and become wanderers through the solar system. All of these asteroids have been given masculine names (usually the names of Greek gods and heroes) and are referred to collectively as the male asteroids. The male asteroids do not really wander. They too orbit the sun, but their orbits cut across the orbits of other planets, including the orbit of earth. And some of these asteroids can come pretty close to earth.

In 1968 the close approach of an asteroid called Icarus set off a small, but very definite end-of-the-world scare. There had already been rumors that a series of worldwide cataclysms was going to begin in 1968. When news that Icarus was heading toward earth and was going to make its closest approach on June 15, 1968, got around, it somehow became combined with the other end-of-the-world rumors. In California groups of hippies headed for the mountains of Colorado saying that they wanted to be safe on high ground before the asteroid hit and caused California to sink into the sea.

If the asteroid actually was to hit the earth there would have been no way of knowing exactly where it would strike. Colorado was really no safer than California, but people

Oblique view of the far side of the moon, photographed from Apollo 11, shows craters in dramatic relief. Scientists are still not sure how many of the moon's craters were formed by meteorite impacts and how many by volcanic action. *N.A.S.A.*

who are gripped by a fear that the world is about to end rarely act logically. Perhaps the flight to Colorado was more of a put-on than anything else, but it did get a lot of publicity. Plenty of people who did not run to Colorado in 1968 awaited June 15 with some foreboding.

But anyone who thought that he would awaken on the morning of June 15 and see the great mass of Icarus rushing through the sky was disappointed—and doubtless relieved. As a sky show, the close approach of Icarus was a complete fizzle, as astronomers knew it would be. Icarus was really much too far and much too small to be seen with the naked eye. Unlike comets which vaporize and glow brilliantly, asteroids do not vaporize, do not glow, and are hard to locate. Icarus could be traced only with difficulty by the radars of the Deep Space Network in the Mohave Desert. If Icarus had been a comet it would have been the brightest object in the sky.

The orbit of Icarus is as well-known as the orbit of any of the male asteroids. The orbit was first determined in 1949. Icarus' orbit carries it inside the orbit of Mercury and to within 17 million miles of the surface of the sun—hence the name Icarus, after the Greek mythological figure who flew too close to the sun. The asteroid then swings around and heads for the outer reaches of the solar system. It makes one complete circuit every nineteen years; thus every nineteen years it is in the vicinity of the earth.

The astronomers knew that Icarus was coming, and they were watching for it. They did not believe that the asteroid would strike the earth in 1968. But in 1965 Dr. Robert S. Richardson, formerly of the Mount Wilson Observatory in California, wrote an article in which he cited the "remote possibility" that the asteroid might someday hit the earth. Dr. Richardson wrote, "A change of only a few degrees

Craters on the surface of Mars photographed by Mariner 7. N.A.S.A.

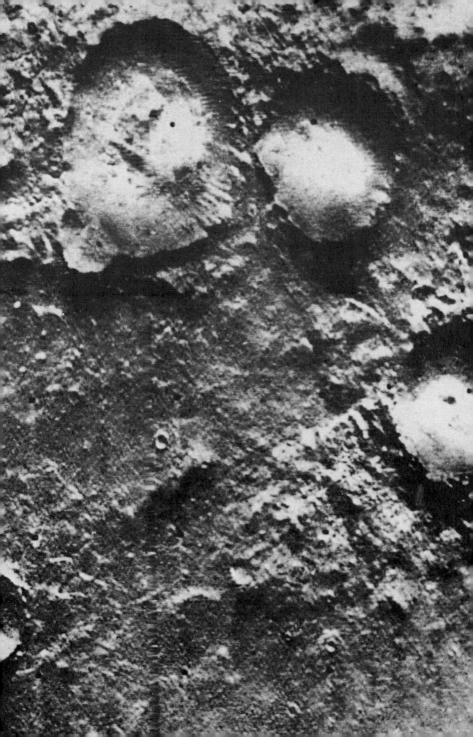

in the position of the descending node of Icarus' orbit, the point at which the asteroid crosses the plane of earth's orbit from north to south, would make it possible for Icarus and the earth to be at the same place at the same time." This was not a prediction, but it was quite enough to start some people worrying.

From Rome came a story that the Vatican Observatory was trying to calculate the exact spot at which the asteroid would hit. This story was a hoax, but that was not discovered until it had appeared in the newspapers around the world.

A group of American students began a project in which they tried to calculate how the asteroid could be blown up by nuclear missiles before it actually collided with earth. This was simply an imaginative class exercise, not a serious attempt to save the world, but it too fed the doomsday fears.

Then came a report that an Australian scientist had called for a meeting of all the great powers to work out a plan to destroy Icarus before it hit earth.

Most astronomers were puzzled or angered by the excitement. They pointed out that Icarus had been close to earth before, closer, in fact, than it was scheduled to come in 1968. Besides, thirty years before there had been a series of much closer passes by large asteroids. The asteroid Apollo came within 2 million miles of earth in 1932. Adonis was within a million miles in 1936. In 1937 there was some genuine concern among astronomers when Hermes skimmed within a mere 485,000 miles of earth on October 30. That was still twice as far away as the moon, but it was the closest known approach of an asteroid to earth.

Apollo, Adonis, and Hermes, like Icarus, are each about a mile in diameter. Hermes has an estimated mass of 3,000 million tons. Back in 1898 the asteroid Eros which is fifteen miles in diameter caused a stir by coming close to the earth.

Eros is the largest asteroid known to enter the vicinity of the earth.

Astronomers know a good deal less about the comings and goings of the male asteroids than you might suspect. In space an object a mile or two in diameter and reflecting only a faint light is hard to find. By the time the asteroids come close enough to be seen they are going so fast across the sky that it requires a good deal of luck to keep track of them. Astronomers were able to keep a watch on Icarus because they knew its orbit and thus knew where to look for it. But we do not know the exact orbits of Apollo, Adonis, and Hermes, so we don't know where they are now or when they will again make a close pass at earth. Besides, it is very difficult to calculate the orbits of bodies as small as the asteroids, because the orbits are often perturbed by passing the larger planets.

Dr. Richardson said, "We are aware of these close-approaching asteroids only through the accident of discovery. No one knows how many objects ranging in size from a few miles in diameter downward may pass near the earth each year without being noticed."

Most meteorites either burn up in the atmosphere or get slowed down so that they hit the earth with a comparatively gentle impact. But anything weighing over a thousand tons would hardly be slowed at all, and might slam into the earth at a speed of up to thirty-seven miles per second.

What would happen to earth if an asteroid a mile or more in diameter hit earth at that speed? It would be a disaster, everyone is agreed about that. But there is a great deal of uncertainty regarding how large and what kind of a disaster it would be. We simply have no experience with an earthly cataclysm of that magnitude so we have nothing to compare it with.

1949 MA (BAADE OBJECT)   10'

The arrow points to a thin white line that represents the path
of the asteroid Icarus. Though Icarus created a minor end-of-
the-world scare on earth, it was barely detectable even to the
most sensitive astronomical equipment. *Mount Wilson and
Palomar Observatories*

Model showing the comparative size of the asteroid Hermes
and Manhattan Island. *Courtesy of the American Museum of
Natural History*

Dr. Gerald Hawkins of Harvard Observatory ran some figures through a computer and came up with these conclusions: a 55-million-ton meteorite with a diameter of a mere 1,700 feet striking earth at a moderate speed would blast out a hole 6.12 miles across. And that is a large meteorite, not an asteroid. One estimate was that if Icarus collided with earth it would have the destructive potential of seven thousand 100-megaton thermonuclear bombs.

Dr. Harold Masursky of the U.S. Geological Survey believes that an asteroid the size of Icarus would blast out a crater as large as the crater Copernicus on the moon. Copernicus is sixty miles across and two miles deep. Cliffs a thousand feet high ring the rim of the crater.

Such an impact would not go unfelt anywhere on the earth. Bad atmospheric disturbances would circle the globe. A lot would depend upon where the asteroid struck. If it hit anywhere near a population center the loss of life would be far higher than if it slammed into the Siberian taiga. Most likely, however, an asteroid or anything else hitting earth would land in the ocean simply because three quarters of the earth's surface is covered with water. An asteroid hitting the ocean would create a *tsunami* (tidal wave) of such monstrous size that it would probably swamp all the islands and low-lying coastal areas on the ocean's rim.

Dr. Masursky is one of those scientists who believes that large impacts are more frequent than is commonly believed by his colleagues. He suggests that science pay serious attention to these potential cosmic bombs. He has suggested tracking the male asteroids more closely so that we could get sufficient advance warning if one of them was about to hit the earth. Then rockets with nuclear warheads could be launched to blow the asteroid into relatively harmless fragments, before it hit the earth.

Icarus and the rest and even Eros with its fifteen-mile diameter are still fairly small asteroids. We know that much larger asteroids orbit in the asteroid belt, and we can not be entirely sure that larger ones do not also cut through the orbits of other planets, including earth. None have been detected so far but, as we pointed out, they are hard to detect. Nor do we have the faintest idea what pushes an asteroid out of the belt and sets it careening through the solar system.

What would happen if something really big, a hundred miles across or more, struck the earth? How big a crater would such an object make? It would dig a crater about the size of the Pacific Ocean, and one theory holds that such a collision is indeed responsible for the formation of the ocean basin.

For a long time some scientists contended that a huge chunk of matter was torn from the earth's surface when the planet was young. The chunk itself was caught in orbit around the earth and became the moon. The resulting scar on the earth's surface became the Pacific Ocean. This theory, however, has lost favor among scientists, and few consider it seriously today.

Then in 1960 a British scientist, Dr. E. R. Harrison theorized that just the opposite happened. Sometime early in the earth's history an asteroid about 120 miles in diameter smashed into the earth and formed a crater 100 miles deep and thousands of miles in diameter.

The force of such a blow would have wobbled the earth in its orbit, set off a terrific amount of volcanic activity and shifted the crust of the entire earth. When the violent reactions had died down the original crater would be partially filled in, and it would look like some of the large shallow craters seen on the moon. These moon craters are called seas although they contain no water and probably never did.

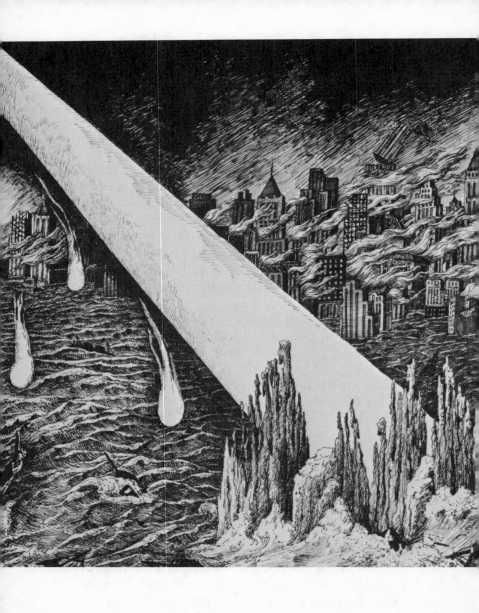

An imaginary representation of the fall of an asteroid into lower New York. *Courtesy of the American Museum of Natural History*

Dr. Harrison calculated that the force of such an impact would be roughly equivalent to that produced if a twenty-kiloton atomic bomb was exploded over every square yard of the impact area.

Another result of the impact would be that all or most of the earth's atmosphere would be blasted out into space.

Ultimately a new atmosphere would form, and erosion and mountain building would erase the more characteristic features of the impact crater, making the Pacific Ocean virtually unrecognizable as a crater. Dr. Harrison even suggested that all of the major seas and oceans of the earth might have been formed as the result of collisions with large asteroids.

This theory gained little support when it was first proposed. In the years since 1960 other theories about the formation of the ocean basins have become very popular among scientists, and so the idea that the Pacific Ocean is really a gigantic impact crater is probably less acceptable now than it was when it was first proposed.

Still, in subjects like this scientists are speculating at the very edges of human knowledge. There is little that we know for certain about the formation of the earth and its major features. Though it is highly unlikely that the Pacific Ocean basin is really a gigantic impact crater, it is not entirely impossible.

In any event this speculation gives us some idea of what might happen if the earth at some future date did collide with a really large asteroid. Not only would every living thing in the impact zone be killed, but every living thing on earth would die as a result. Even if men could somehow survive the shock waves, the earthquakes, tidal waves, and volcanic action that would be the immediate result of the impact they would die anyway because the collision would have the force to knock the earth's atmosphere right out into space. That truly would spell the end of the world.

How likely is such an end? Not very. It is certainly not worth losing sleep over. We don't even know if any asteroids a hundred miles or more in diameter ever get within the vicinity of the earth.

But still Dr. Harrison, looking at the rugged lands that rim part of the Pacific, thought that he could see the weather-worn remains of debris blasted out of a crater made by an asteroid.

And finally what about the asteroid belt itself? Could the planet that should be there have been blasted to bits by a collision with something else? Might that be earth's fate too? We simply do not know.

CHAPTER 6

Extinction!

Oh, gaze upon this model beast,
Defunct ten million years at least.
—BERT L. TAYLOR

Our species, *Homo sapiens*, is remarkably self-centered and shortsighted. We go to the museum and look at the gigantic skeletons of the dinosaurs, and this makes us feel very smug.

"How big and clumsy they were," we say. "Despite their size and all their armor and teeth they died out. How overspecialized and poorly adapted for survival in a changing world they were! What perfect candidates for extinction." When we want to characterize something as big, unworkable, and headed for the scrap heap we call it a dinosaur.

After returning from the museum we might gaze into the mirror to contemplate our own relatively small and unspecialized form. We have stubby, blunt teeth and nails and no armor plate at all. Yet weak and helpless as we may appear, we are alive, and all that is left of the dinosaurs is a mass of fossilized bones. Unlike the giant reptiles, we think, we are not going to lumber off to an early extinction because we are too big or too heavily armored to cope with the world. We're adaptable, and we're smart. Dinosaurs were overspecialized and stupid.

This sort of comparison between man and dinosaur has been made many times and it makes us feel good. But it is false and misleading. We are a relatively new species. Something vaguely akin to man may have existed for under 2 million years. Our own particular species is less than a million years old.

The dinosaurs ruled the earth—and that is no flight of rhetorical fancy—they literally ruled the earth for 100 million years. If our kind survives for another 98 million years we may then be able to compare our success to that of the dinosaurs.

The dinosaurs have now been dead and gone for some 70 million years. If the dinosaurs had not died out the mammals—and we are mammals—would never have become as large and varied a class as they are today. In fact, man would probably never have evolved at all if our ancestors had to compete with dinosaurs. There were mammals around during the millions of years of dinosaurian dominance, but they remained small and insignificant until the dinosaurs were out of the way. Only after the giant reptiles had disappeared from the earth were the mammals able to become an evolutionary success. Still, it took millions of years for the mammals to take over the empty ecological niches left by the dead dinosaurs.

This brings up the question of why the dinosaurs died out in the first place. The answer is that we simply do not know. But something very strange and possibly very terrible happened to that tribe of great reptiles. "They all went,"

These are some of the types of dinosaurs that lived during the late Cretaceous period, the end of the Age of Reptiles. The reason for the sudden extinction of these great reptiles remains unknown. *Courtesy of the American Museum of Natural History*

wrote the Canadian paleontologist W. E. Swinton, "without a single survivor or descendant." Not one of today's reptiles can count the dinosaurs among their direct ancestors.

The extinction of the dinosaurs was mysterious and, as far as we can tell, very sudden. The event has been called the Great Death. What is more there seem to have been other periods of Great Death in the history of the earth. One occurred at the end of the Permian period, just before the rise of the dinosaurs. At that time many of the dominant species seem to have died off suddenly. That is why we are discussing dinosaurs in a book about the end of the world.

The Great Death has happened before, and it might happen again. And the next time the victims may be men.

Let us look more closely at the Great Death of the dinosaurs. The word "dinosaur" means "terrible lizard." The word is a bit misleading because dinosaurs were not lizards and not all of them were terrible, though many certainly were. The dinosaurs were a large and extremely varied group of land-living reptiles ranging in size from small birdlike creatures to the gigantic sauropods like Brontosaurus and Diplodocus, the largest land animals that have ever lived. During the 100 million years of dinosaurian dominance many different species, indeed entire groups of dinosaurs, became extinct and new ones evolved. But the dinosaurs as a group flourished right up to the end of the period of earth history called the Cretaceous, the time of the Great Death. The heavily armored stegosaurs were already extinct, the gigantic sauropods were significantly reduced in numbers. But there were huge herds of duckbill dinosaurs, and the smaller swifter dinosaurs were more numerous than ever. The remains of these dinosaurs abound in the rocks of the late Cretaceous. Then the dinosaurs simply drop out of the fossil record, and scientists assume that they become extinct.

Paleontologist Dr. Edwin H. Colbert, one of the world's leading experts on dinosaurs has written, "Not one of them survived into a later geologic age, as is amply proved by the fact that during almost a century and a half of paleontological exploration, the wide world over, no trace of a dinosaur bone or tooth has ever been found in any post-Cretaceous rocks, not even in the earliest of them. The proof of the geologic record on this score is irrefutable."

Alas, there is not a shred of substance to all of those wonderful and romantic tales of dinosaurs that still live on some isolated island, or in the midst of a remote jungle. The dinosaurs are dead and gone and have been for 70 million years.

The dinosaurs were not the only animals to disappear at the end of the Cretaceous. The seas of the Cretaceous had also been dominated by huge reptiles, the mosasaurs and plesiosaurs. The largest flying creatures of the Cretaceous were also reptiles—the pterosaurs. But at the end of the Cretaceous all of these creatures like the dinosaurs themselves disappear from the fossil record. The entire order of reptiles was drastically reduced from fifty known families at the end of the Cretaceous to a mere fifteen at the beginning of the next geological period. Since that time the reptiles have recovered somewhat, and there are more different kinds of reptiles today, than there were in the years following the Great Death. At that same time a number of small marine invertebrates, which had been extremely common also became extinct.

There are some very peculiar things about this wave of extinctions. While all of the dinosaurs, large and small died off, the lizards and crocodiles did not. The mosasaurs and plesiosaurs vanished from the sea, but the sea turtles continued to thrive. While the pterosaurs disappeared from the skies the very reptile-like archaic birds did not. And the little mammals which had competed so unsuccessfully with the great reptiles also survived.

Says Dr. Colbert, ". . . the problem of extinction is one to which we return, time and again, even though very little is known about it. The most hardheaded and blase geologist is more often than not apt to get excited when he becomes involved in a discussion of the extinction of the dinosaurs."

When we say that the dinosaurs and their allies vanished abruptly, we do not mean to imply that this happened overnight, in a few years, a few hundred or even a few thousand years. We simply do not know how long it took. If a man had been alive to observe the end of the Cretaceous, he might not have been able to notice, in the space of a single human lifetime, that the dinosaurs were dying out. The fossil record can give us only the most general sort of picture. Isolated pockets of dinosaurs might have survived for a couple of million years. But compared to the general slow process of extinction, the disappearance of this large and once successful group seems freakishly abrupt.

The first explanation for the Great Death that springs to mind is that there was some sort of worldwide catastrophe. As we have seen, it was once assumed that all extinctions were the result of worldwide catastrophes. Baron Cuvier would not have felt at all puzzled by the Great Death. But modern scientists are puzzled, because if there had been some sort of worldwide catastrophe there should have been some record of it in the rocks of the Cretaceous. There is none.

"Catastrophes," growls Dr. Colbert, "are the mainstays of people who have very little knowledge of the natural world; for them the invocation of catastrophes is an easy way to explain great events. But the modern student of nature is quite aware that the evolution of the earth and the evolution of life upon the earth have not proceeded by catastrophic events, even though local catastrophes—the eruption of a volcano or the sweep of an epidemic—may temporarily affect the progress of nature in some specific area."

At one time there was a good deal of talk about "racial senescence." Groups of animals, it was thought, went through a youth, maturity, and old age just as an individual does. Then at some point the group died out from "old age." The idea is a rather metaphysical one. If the dinosaurs as a group became "old," why didn't the turtles, which evolved at about the same time and are still around and doing very nicely? Or what about the opossum, which first appeared in the time of the dinosaurs and has remained virtually unchanged to the present day? The theory of "racial senescence" isn't very popular any more.

How about the idea that the dinosaurs became overspecialized and were unable to adapt? But what does "overspecialized" mean? A man who is held underwater will drown, does this mean he is overspecialized because he cannot draw oxygen from the water as a fish does? Then the question arises, What is it that the dinosaurs are supposed to have failed to "adapt" to? Conditions on earth at the end of the Cretaceous had changed greatly from the time the dinosaurs first evolved. During the Cretaceous, particularly the late Cretaceous, there began a series of earth movements which ultimately brought forth our modern mountain chains —the Himalayas, the Andes, the Alps, and the Rockies. Before the mountain building there existed vast shallow inland seas and swamps. But the land masses of the world rose, and these inland seas and swamps receded, and most of them dried up entirely.

We know that the vegetation of the world changed considerably during the Cretaceous. The dinosaurs of the early Cretaceous lived in a world of primitive plants, while those of the late Cretaceous lived amid the sort of plant life we still find on earth today. The climate of the earth may have gotten colder as well although we have no direct evidence of this.

Thus the earth had changed from a place of shallow lakes and swamps filled with soft plants (the kind of world in which we like to picture dinosaurs living) to a place with mountains, high plateaus, and the tougher-to-chew modern plants.

At first glance it would appear that this was the series of changes to which the overspecialized dinosaurs failed to adapt. It is a fine theory, but one is reminded of the saying, "One of the tragedies of life is the murder of a beautiful theory by a brutal gang of facts."

The brutal gang of facts in this case is the overwhelming evidence that the changes in the earth's surface had been taking place slowly over a long period of time. Right up to the end of the Cretaceous the dinosaurs seemed to have been adapting wonderfully to them. Indeed, in the late Cretaceous, while all the mountain building was going on, the dinosaurs flourished as never before, right up to the end of the period. There is no evidence to indicate that anything special happened to make the entire world unfit for dinosaurs. It is reasonable to assume that had the dinosaurs survived the Great Death some of them might still be living in the swamps and jungles of the world today.

This accumulation of changes, particularly the drying

up of the inland seas and the alteration in vegetation, would undoubtedly prove to be too much for many dinosaurs to adapt to successfully. Most susceptible would have been the gigantic plant-eaters who depended upon huge quantities of soft water-plants for food. The larger carnivorous dinosaurs, which preyed upon the large herbivores, would have quickly followed their prey to extinction. One cannot imagine the fearsome Tyrannosaurus sustaining itself on a diet of small game. But these changes cannot easily account for the extinction of the small dinosaurs and the marine reptiles and pterosaurs. And what killed off those marine invertebrates that suddenly drop out of the fossil record?

All manner of variations of the climatic-change theory have been proposed. Perhaps the cause of the Great Death of the dinosaurs lies in a subtle and little-understood interaction of relatively minor and slow changes. But no one is quite satisfied with this explanation. The notion persists, that the earth, despite Dr. Colbert's objection, did undergo some sort of catastrophic change at the end of the Cretaceous and at other periods as well. But the catastrophe could not have been the traditional one of worldwide flood, massive earthquakes, or vastly increased volcanic activity. That sort of catastrophe would show up in the geological record.

In recent years it has been proposed that the extinction of the dinosaurs and other waves of mass extinctions have come about when the earth was suddenly bombarded by a burst of penetrating and deadly radiation from space. Radiation in very high doses can kill directly. Far lower doses can damage a creature's reproductive organs and render it sterile. At still lower doses radiation produces a high number of stillbirths and mutations. Mutations are generally harmful and lower the survival potential of a species.

Two possible ways in which the radiation hitting the

The Crab Nebula, the remains of a supernova that was first observed by Chinese astronomers in A.D. 1054. Today this large cloud of gas is expanding outward at a speed of 1000 miles per second. *Mount Wilson and Palomar Observatories.*

earth could have been increased dramatically and disastrously have been proposed. The theory that has received the most attention concerns the appearance of a nearby supernova.

A supernova is the most spectacular thing that happens in our galaxy. The first recorded observation of a supernova from earth appears in the *Records* of the Royal Observatory of Peking.

"In the first year of the period Chihha, the fifth moon the day Chi-chou [July 4, 1054, in our calendar] a great star appeared approximately several inches southeast of T'ien-Kuan [Zeta Tauri on modern star charts]. After more than a year it gradually became invisible."

This "great star" is not invisible to modern astronomers. They have located its remains, a peculiar astronomical object called the Crab Nebula, so named because it is found in the constellation of Cancer the crab. The Crab Nebula is a great expanding cloud of luminous gas. It is expanding at a rate of a thousand miles a second. This cloud of gas is all that remains of a large star that exploded. Though the Crab Nebula was known for a long time, it was only about thirty years ago that astronomers associated it with the "great star" that had suddenly appeared to the Chinese.

The explosion of a small star is called a *nova*. The word means "new star." In the past when a star suddenly flared brightly in the sky, it looked like the birth of a new star rather than the explosion of a dying one.

What had happened in 1054 was that the Chinese had witnessed the cataclysmic explosion of a large star far out in space. Astronomers estimate that for the Chinese to have seen this very distant explosion so clearly it must have been almost a billion times as brilliant as our own sun. Other peoples must have seen the "new star" too, but they made no record of it. The brightness has been compared to the combined brightness of all the stars in the Milky Way. Such explosions are so much greater than novas that they are called *supernovas*, "super new stars."

We don't know exactly what causes a supernova, though numerous theories have been advanced to explain the event. In general it is assumed that the supernova is the last stage in the death of a very large star. The star begins to collapse in upon itself under the force of its own weight.

The heat generated by the collapse drives the central temperature of the star up to 100 billion degrees, and this releases a chain of different nuclear reactions. The result is an explosion which blows the star into an expanding cloud of radioactive gas and dust.

Since the supernova observed by the Chinese in 1054 there have been two other supernovas recorded by astronomers. One took place in 1572 in the constellation of Cassiopeia and was described by Tycho Brahe. Astonishingly a mere thirty-two years later another supernova became visible and a description of it was recorded by Brahe's famous former assistant Johannes Kepler. Since that time there have been no new supernovas observed. However, supernovas also occur in other stellar systems or galaxies, and the remains of the supernovas are bright enough to be identified with powerful telescopes. During the last seventy-five years some two hundred supernovas have been photographed with telescopes. In 1972 California astronomer Charles Kowal spotted the remains of a supernova in a nearby galaxy.

So while supernovas are rare celestial events, they are not all that rare. Physicist George Gamow estimates that one occurs in our own galaxy, the Milky Way, about every three hundred years. He comments, "The time is ripe for the next one."

In the view of the Russian theoretical astronomer Dr. Iosif Shklovskii, the time is not merely ripe, it is overripe. Dr. Shklovskii is known for his willingness to step in and speculate boldly where more cautious astronomers fear to tread. Along with a colleague, Dr. R. Minkowski, Dr. Shklovskii has examined objects in our galaxy that seem to be the remnants of supernovas. On the basis of this study the two Russian astronomers estimate that supernovas occur in our galaxy about once every fifty years, or about six times as often as previously believed. Some supernovas would be so far away that they would escape the detection of astronomers and might be discovered only by accident. A really huge supernova, like the one which created the Crab Nebula would, of course, be visible to everyone.

The more common the supernova event, the more likely it is that one could take place nearby. Now "nearby" to Dr. Shklovskii means within ten parsecs, an astronomical unit of distance. One parsec equals approximately 3.26 light years. Thus ten parsecs would be about thirty-three light years. For comparison the Crab Nebula is thirteen hundred light years away from earth, and Dr. Kowal's supernova about 10 million light years away.

Dr. Shklovskii envisions this kind of scenario for a nearby supernova. The explosion lights up the night sky. It is a million times brighter than the brightest star, and forty times brighter than the moon. After several months the great and ominous glow in the sky begins to fade. But the faintly luminous gas blown out by the explosion continues to expand through space and toward the earth. Some ten thousand years or so after the original explosion became visible the gas cloud reaches earth bringing with it a bombardment of cosmic rays that would last for tens of thousands of years.

During this period all of the living creatures on earth would be subjected to a barrage of cosmic rays ten times as intense as under normal conditions. What would happen? We need only look at the survivors of the atomic bombs at Hiroshima and Nagasaki to get some idea of what the long-term effects of radiation can be. There would be no disfiguring radiation burns, but the mutations, stillbirths, and cancer would occur. Over a period of time these destructive effects could bring about the extinction of certain species. Dr. Shklovskii thinks that the radiation from a nearby supernova explosion might have been the thing that did in the dinosaurs.

By chance astronomers were able to photograph the death of a star. The photo at left shows an ordinary star, but a photo of the same star taken a few days later shows the explosion into a nova. *Lick Observatory*

Naturally many disagree with Dr. Shklovskii's theory. Why they ask, did radiation kill off dinosaurs, but not lizards and crocodiles, why mosasaurs and plesiosaurs and not turtles and why pterosaurs and not birds? The answer might be, simply, pure chance. During the bombardment of radiation the total populations of all species would have been reduced markedly. When the radiation ended some species would have the ability or luck to recover, while others would totter off to extinction. Large animals that depend on a high individual survival rate would be most susceptible to extinction under such conditions.

Different forms of life have markedly different levels of resistance to radiation. A radiation dose that would kill a man would hardly faze a cockroach. There is no way of knowing whether the dinosaurs and the other large reptiles of the Cretaceous were more susceptible to radiation damage than those animals that survived.

The destructive effects of the radiation need not have been direct. Dr. G. M. Woodwell of Brookhaven National Laboratories has done research on the effects that radiation has on the patterns of nature. A large dose of radiation might temporarily disrupt the balance of nature. For example the radiation might drastically reduce the numbers of certain types of plants. The plants being relatively resistant to long-term radiation damage, however, would recover quickly. No change in plant life would show up in the fossil record. But by the time the plants had recovered the dinosaurs that fed upon them might have already starved to death.

The balance of nature, as man is only now beginning to learn, is complex and subtle. The introduction of any new element into this delicate balance may have far reaching and thoroughly unexpected consequences.

Most scientists concerned with dinosaurs or supernovas

are extremely reluctant to endorse the idea that a supernova caused the extinction of the dinosaurs. They contend that we just don't know enough about either subject. But a couple of U.S. scientists have carried the idea even farther out.

Dr. K. D. Terry of the University of Kansas and Dr. W. H. Tucker of Rice University theorize that the radiation from a supernova instead of arriving slowly over tens of thousands of years would all hit the earth in one intense burst. This blast of radiation would last a few days at most.

If the Terry-Tucker thesis is correct it would mean two things: First, a species rather than perishing slowly from an increase in mutations and disease might be wiped out at once by the heavy radiation. Second, and even more ominously as far as the future of mankind is concerned, it would mean that a supernova would be dangerous up to several hundred light years away, not just at the mere thirty-light-year limit estimated by the Russian scientists. The reason for this is that an organism can withstand a large dose of radiation, if the dose is spread over a long period of time. But if the same total amount of radiation is administered quickly, say over a few days, the organism's ability to withstand it without damage is greatly reduced.

A lethal dose of radiation for most laboratory animals ranges between 200 and 900 r (r stands for *roentgens*, a standard unit used to measure radiation). For man the lethal dose ranges between 350 and 600 r. Reptiles seem more resistant to radiation than most mammals. In general, the simpler the organism the better it is able to withstand the detrimental effects of radiation.

Drs. Terry and Tucker estimate that "in the 600 million years since Precambrian times it is probable that at least one supernova occurred producing a dose of 2500 r or more, four producing 1000 r or more, ten with 500 r or more."

Using these figures we can estimate that the earth was probably exposed to a dose of 500 r or more (a dose high enough to cause mass extinctions) about once every 50 million years. According to some estimates waves of mass extinction have swept the earth approximately once every 60 million years. This is a match that Drs. Terry and Tucker think may be "more than coincidental."

The dinosaurs died out some 70 million years ago. That means that there should have been another wave of mass extinctions between that time and the present day. There was, and very recently too—a mere ten thousand years ago. Since we have been tossing about millions and tens of millions of years quite casually, ten thousand years is very recent.

Ten thousand years ago marked the end of the Pleistocene period or Ice Age on earth. Before the end of the Pleistocene an enormous variety of gigantic mammals roamed most of the earth's surface. Elephants and rhinoceroses of various types lived throughout North America and Europe. There were beavers as big as bears and pigs the size of bison. After the Pleistocene most of these giant mammals were gone. Only Africa and the tropical parts of Asia retained a significant number of large mammals. Even in these havens the total number of large species was severely reduced. Most people assume that the glaciers of the Ice Age somehow caused the mass extinctions. But they didn't, nor did any other climatic change, as far as we know.

The timing of the Pleistocene extinctions fits in rather neatly with the supernova theory of extinctions. But this beautiful theory also runs afoul of a brutal gang of facts. The most brutal of these facts is that if a supernova explosion had taken place nearby that recently the remains of the explosion should still be visible. They are not. The nearest supernova remnant is the star designated CTS-1, about four hundred light years away. Four hundred light years is the outer limit at which a dangerous supernova could exist. CTS-1, as far as we can tell, was a very small supernova and damaging radiation from it would never have reached earth.

So a supernova can not be brought in to account for the Pleistocene extinctions, and the reasons for them remain obscure. In the last few years the idea that man was responsible for the mass extinctions of the Pleistocene has become increasingly popular. But this theory is far from universally accepted, and theories about the Pleistocene extinctions can provoke a heated argument among paleontologists.

The supernova theory offered by Drs. Terry and Tucker is really just an estimation of what might have occurred, not an attempt to describe what actually did occur. "The parameters involved in making these calculations are poorly known," they comment.

We simply have no hard evidence that the earth ever was subjected to a huge dose of cosmic radiation from a nearby supernova. Perhaps the theory that all of the radiation from such an explosion would reach earth in a very short period of time is wrong. Perhaps Dr. Shklovskii's estimation of one supernova in our galaxy every fifty years is also wrong. If we abandon these ideas and return to the conventional beliefs about supernovas, then we can stop worrying about them. The chances of one exploding near enough to cause disruptions on earth are so small as to be almost negligible.

Besides even if a supernova were to light up forty times brighter than the moon in tonight's sky, it would still be thousands of years before the dangerous radiation would reach us. We might have some concern about the future of mankind, but we wouldn't have to worry personally. With that much advance warning man might be able to figure out ways to eliminate, or at least minimize the damaging effects of the radiation bombardment. Particularly if the radiation was at a relatively low level and arrived over a long period of time.

It has even been suggested that encounters with supernovas need not be catastrophic at all. There is a theory that every 200 or 300 million years the solar system sails through the gas cloud produced by a supernova. During such a time, cosmic-ray intensity would increase for a period of several thousand years. The increase, however, would be a bearable one. The resulting rise in mutations rather than causing extinctions would act as a spur to evolution.

Even under "normal" conditions, that is, when the earth is not passing through the gas cloud of a supernova, there is plenty of high-energy radiation out in space. Fortunately for us, earth is protected from most of this radiation by its magnetic field.

For centuries it has been known that the earth acts like a gigantic magnet. It is the earth's magnetism that causes the needle of a compass to point north. But it was not until man was able to probe space with artificial satellites that he realized how important the magnetic field is. The earth's magnetic field extends far out into space. Instruments aboard the satellites showed that a significant proportion of the radiation out in space is trapped by the earth's magnetic field and prevented from reaching the surface of the earth. This was one of the major discoveries of the early years of the space age.

Just exactly how the earth's magnetic field is created, and why it acts as it does, is unknown. As usual there is no lack of theories, but a group of scientists working in the field of magnetism summed up the situation this way: "After centuries of research the earth's magnetic field remains one of the best-described and least understood of all planetary phenomena."

Recently scientists have made discoveries about earth's magnetic field that compound the puzzle. The magnetic field, it seems, does not remain constant, it regularly reverses itself. The magnetic north pole becomes the magnetic south pole and vice versa. Such reversals appear to have taken place at least nine times in the last 4 million years.

That the earth's magnetic field is not stable has been known for hundreds of years, that it actually reverses itself is a relatively recent discovery. The discovery was so unexpected that scientists at first refused to accept the evidence. But the evidence was there in the rocks of the earth. The alteration in the earth's magnetic field, like the changes in life itself has left a fossil record.

The earth's magnetic field is relatively weak, but it is strong enough to magnetize certain types of volcanic rocks while they are molten. When these rocks harden, they contain a record of the direction of the magnetic field at the time of their formation.

In 1906 a French physicist named Bernard Brunhes noted that the polarity of some ancient rocks was the exact reverse of today's polarity. It seemed as though the positions of the north and south magnetic poles had been switched at the time that the ancient rocks were formed. Brunhes suggested that the earth's magnetic field had once reversed itself. At the time the idea seemed preposterous, and nobody paid any attention to it.

In 1929 the Japanese geophysicist Montonori Matuyama found that the volcanic rocks of the early Pleistocene about 700,000 years ago showed polarity in reverse of what it is today. This evidence supported the contention first advanced by Brunhes. The evidence was piling up and couldn't be so easily brushed aside. Since that time evidence that the earth's magnetic field has reversed itself, not once but several times, has become overwhelming. Today the idea which once seemed absurd is generally accepted. Nobody can explain why this reversal occurs, though numerous attempts at explanations have been made.

The reasons for the magnetic reversal need not concern us here. What does concern us, however, is what happens during one of these reversals. A complete switch in the magnetic field seems to take about five thousand years. During the switchover period the magnetic field gradually weakens, until at the midpoint it is a bare 5 or 6 percent of its normal strength. Then it builds up again in the other direction. Since the earth's magnetic field is our main protection against cosmic rays, any reduction in this field would result in a major increase in cosmic radiation hitting the earth.

For an estimated five hundred years around the time of the magnetic polarity change, the earth's magnetic field would be so weak, that cosmic rays would be able to bombard the earth almost unhampered. What would the effects of such a bombardment be? We don't really know, of course, but there are the gloomy prospects of an increase in mutations and the possible extinction of species.

Dr. R. J. Uffen, a Canadian geophysicist, was one of the first scientists to suggest that these magnetic reversals, with their accompanying jumps in cosmic radiation might be the reasons for the periodic mass extinctions.

This idea was almost as startling as the idea that the earth's magnetic field reversed itself. But evidence supporting Dr. Uffen's theory began turning up in the mid 1960s. Oceanographers with drilling rigs brought up core samples of deep-sea sediment. These sediments were laid down at different periods of time and they contained fossils of the marine animals that had lived during the time. From such samples it was possible for scientists to get a fair idea of what sorts of creatures had lived in the ocean over the past few million years.

Oceanographers at the Lamont-Doherty Geological Observatory of Columbia University noted that about 2.5 million years ago a large number of species of algae and protozoa seemed to appear suddenly in the fossil record found in the cores. About 2.5 million years ago there is evidence that a magnetic reversal took place.

Dr. James D. Hays of Lamont studied deep-sea cores from twenty-eight different locations around the world. He found that 700,000 years ago six species of a one-celled marine animal called Radiolaria simultaneously became extinct across their entire range. The odds that such a simultaneous extinction might take place entirely by chance are about 1 in 10,000, Dr. Hays estimates. Recall that Matuyama discovered that 700,000 years ago was the time of another magnetic reversal.

This evidence linking past magnetic reversals with periods of mass extinction or with evolutionary spurts is interesting but at best it is scanty and at times even contradictory. There is, as yet, no way of linking the death of the dinosaurs to a reversal of the earth's magnetic field, because our evidence on earth's magnetic field goes back only a few million years. The dinosaurs became extinct 70 million years ago. The last great wave of extinctions was at the end of the Pleistocene, ten thousand years ago. But at that time there was no magnetic reversal. Obviously mass extinctions can take place without a magnetic reversal.

Some scientists, while believing that the magnetic reversals have changed the course of evolution on this planet, do not believe that the increase in cosmic radiation is the agent responsible for the change.

Dr. Hays believes that the magnetic field itself has a direct effect upon animal life. He points out that experiments have shown that certain animals such as snails and bees are

sensitive to magnetic fields. Why, however, a reverse magnetic field should cause some species to die out remains
unexplained.

Still another idea, proposed by Drs. James P. Kennett and
Norman D. Watkins of the University of Rhode Island, is
that the magnetic reversal triggers intense geologic activity,
including volcanic eruptions. The dust from these explosions
would be thrown into the atmosphere forming a cloud that
would temporarily block radiation from the sun and thus
bring about major climatic changes, which in turn might bring
about mass extinction.

What sort of effect might a magnetic reversal have on
our own species, *Homo sapiens?* We really don't know, because we have never been through one. At the time of the
last magnetic reversal 700,000 years ago there were no *Homo
sapiens* on earth. However, one of the new species to appear
at about that time was *Homo erectus,* one of our very own
ancestors. We don't have nearly enough evidence to attribute
the evolution of *Homo erectus* to the magnetic reversal. But
it's something to think about.

We, or rather our descendants, may have a first-hand
opportunity to find out what a magnetic reversal will do to
Homo sapiens. All the evidence indicates that the earth's
magnetic field is weakening. It is down about 15 percent since
1670. A study made by the U.S. Coast and Geodetic Survey
suggests that the magnetic field will reach its minimum
around the year 3991. We should begin feeling the major
effects of the reduction of the magnetic field around the year
3700.

What will these effects be? An increase in radiation with
a resultant rise in mutations, stillbirths, and cancer can almost
be counted upon. Will this mean the end of the world or at
least the end of man? We really don't know.

Obviously the problem is not an immediate one. The year A.D. 3700 is a millennia and three quarters from the present day. A millennia and three quarters ago the Emperor Decius had just instituted the first general persecution of Christians at Rome. A lot can happen in a millennia and three quarters. Perhaps we will discover that this linking of mass extinctions and magnetic reversals is an illusion based on incomplete or poorly understood data. Perhaps we will find ways to shield ourselves from the dangerous effects of such reversals, if they do indeed take place. We may find that increase in radiation will not be great enough to have any major effect upon us. There are numerous species that have continued virtually unchanged over the last four million years, a period in which it has been estimated that there have been at least nine magnetic reversals.

On the other hand, in one story about the earth's magnetism, the reporter quoted the remark of an unnamed geologist, "I don't want to be an alarmist," he said, "but man may go the way of the dinosaurs."

CHAPTER 7

The Four Horseman

> And I looked, and behold a pale horse: and his name that sat on him was Death, and Hell followed with him.
>
> —REVELATIONS 6:8

One of the most striking and memorable images in the apocalyptic Book of Revelation is that of the four horsemen. As the book with seven seals is opened seal by seal there is the sound of thunder and four riders appear. They are often referred to as the four horsemen of the apocalypse.

The meaning of the first of the horsemen, seated upon a white horse, is unclear. Some think that this horseman is supposed to be a symbol of Christ, others disagree. But there is little doubt about the meanings of the other three horsemen.

The rider on the red horse is war, the rider on the black horse famine, and the rider on the pale horse death, probably in the form of plague or pestilence. Thus three powerful symbols of the end of the world were great wars, great famines, and great epidemics.

In biblical times the three were often interconnected, wars brought about famines and epidemics. But none of these "three horsemen" was actually looked upon as the agent of worldwide destruction. In the end the sky would open up and God would purge the world with fire. The earthly disorders, no matter how destructive, were merely signs of the coming end.

But in the modern world, war, famine, and pestilence have taken on terrible new meanings. Today the possibility exists that any of these disasters might in itself bring about the end of the world.

War has become progressively more horrible since biblical times. Not that man is any more cruel today than he was two thousand years ago, he just has more efficient weapons. The most sadistic and depraved Roman soldier could not in a lifetime of warfare kill and maim as many people, as a modern bombardier can on a single mission.

The very real possibility that man might completely destroy himself became apparent on August 6, 1945, when a U.S. bomber dropped an atomic bomb on the Japanese city of Hiroshima. The city was destroyed and thousands of people were killed instantly in the blast. Many more died later from radiation burns or other injuries. A second and more powerful atomic bomb was dropped three days later over the city of Nagasaki.

Thus in a flash of blinding light and searing heat did the atomic age open. It was a scene to rival the frenzied visions of the most apocalyptic of biblical prophets.

In the United States the news that atomic bombs had been dropped on Japan produced an immediate sense of euphoria. It seemed that the bombings had brought the war with Japan to an early end and made the United States the number-one power in the world. No one would ever again dare to go to war with the nation that possessed the atomic bomb.

The mood changed rapidly. Soon after the war the other great power in the world, the Soviet Union, developed its own atomic bomb. The United States and the Soviet Union were plunged deep into a cold war that threatened at any moment to erupt into a hot war, and, in this case, a nuclear war. To many, nuclear war seemed inevitable, and the outcome of such a war it seemed would almost certainly be the end of the world.

This author grew up as part of the cold war generation. In my grammar-school newspaper for the fall of 1949 there was a "class prophecy." Such "prophecies" were little stories that were supposed to predict what was going to happen to members of the class in the future. In this case the story was built around what was supposed to happen to all the class members after the next war.

The end of the "prophecy" found a lone survivor hiding in a deep underground tomb carving out the story of the war on rocks, "for posterity."

"However," the "prophecy" concludes, "there naturally were no future generations."

The incident was not untypical. Most Americans growing up during the late 1940s and early 1950s believed that there was going to be a cataclysmic nuclear war within their life-time. Perhaps it is part of human nature or at least the nature of Western man for every generation to grow up believing that it is the last generation in history. Perhaps only the method by which the end is to be brought about changes. In any case, for my generation the feared agent of the destruc-tion of the world was a nuclear war. We believed deeply and passionately that there would be such a war, and like the early Christians we were sure that this Judgment Day would come within our own lifetimes.

Oddly, the development of the infinitely more powerful and destructive hydrogen bomb, by both the United States and the Soviet Union in the early 1950s reassured some people. William L. Lawrence was the science editor for *The New York Times*. He had witnessed the first secret tests of the atomic bomb and was terribly frightened by the implications of the weapon. But Lawrence found the hydrogen bomb to be so indescribably destructive that he was sure that it would make war between the great powers "unthinkable." This was the "balance of terror."

Most people were not at all reassured by the hydrogen bomb. They had heard the prediction that war was unthinkable before. The pacifistically inclined inventor Alfred Nobel who developed dynamite hoped that his invention might make war so terrible that it would become unthinkable. Dynamite made war more terrible, but not unthinkable.

World War I had been so much worse than any one imagined that it would be, that some freely predicted no nation would be insane enough to go to war again. The prediction was quite wrong, as we all know.

In the early 1960s there was an attempt made in the United States to get people to "think about the unthinkable" possibilities of a thermonuclear war. People were told that a high percentage of the population of the United States could survive a major hydrogen bomb attack if they were properly prepared for it. People were urged to build bomb shelters, and a huge civil defense program was launched. There were even mock air raids, just as there had been during World War II.

The project never got off the ground. Many scientists denounced the whole effort as both foolish and dangerous. The bomb shelters would not work, they said, and any attempt to make people believe that thermonuclear war would not be so bad after all would merely encourage governments to start one. The public seemed to agree. Very few private bomb shelters were ever built. Those civil defense programs that got beyond the planning stage faltered and died quickly from lack of public support. People ignored or openly defied the air-raid drill orders. The general attitude seemed to be that the whole civil defense program was a waste of time and money and that even if some survived a thermonuclear war, life would not really be worth living anyway. There is little talk of bomb shelters and civil defense today.

More than a quarter of a century has passed since the first atomic bombs were dropped over Hiroshima and Nagasaki. It has not been a peaceful quarter century, but at least there has been no thermonuclear war much to the surprise (and delight) of this author and many of his contemporaries. The acute tensions between the two great nuclear powers have even died down somewhat. But all is not rosy. Five countries now possess nuclear weapons, and the possibility exists that any technically advanced country could easily and quickly manufacture its own hydrogen bombs if it so desired.

To a certain extent we have learned to live with the bomb and its implications. Diplomatic efforts are now being made to control the future development and spread of nuclear weapons. These efforts have a long way to go, but it is at least a beginning. It is doubtful that during the 1970s there will be many class prophecies written envisioning the imminent end of the world—through nuclear war, anyway.

The almost comfortable familiarity we have established with nuclear weapons over the last quarter-century may be misleading. The weapons are still there, and they are far more dangerous and destructive than those which existed in the late 1940s and early 1950s. Could it happen, could the world be brought to an end by thermonuclear war? The problem falls into two parts, technical and what we might call psychological or political.

The Four Horsemen of the Apocalypse. *New York Public Library Picture Collection*

We know that the two major nuclear powers possess more than enough nuclear explosives to blast every single person off the face of the earth several times over. But it is unlikely that even the worst conceivable nuclear war would have this particular result. Countries that were not directly involved in the war would probably be spared entirely from bombings. Thus there almost certainly would be survivors in large parts of South America, Africa, and Asia. Even in those countries directly hit by bombs there would probably be survivors, perhaps even a significant number of them.

Civilization as we know it would be badly disrupted if not completely destroyed. But the human race would survive —at least for a while.

The element of uncertainty in human survival is introduced because nuclear weapons spread radioactivity in the atmosphere. Besides war on this scale would do an enormous amount of environmental damage even without the radioactivity. No part of the world would remain unaffected by a major thermonuclear war.

Just how much radioactivity would be spread by a war is quite unknown. We cannot predict the course of a future war, nor can we know exactly what kinds of weapons will be used. The early hydrogen bombs produced an enormous amount of radioactive fallout. Since that time scientists and technicians have labored to produce "clean" nuclear weapons. That is, weapons that can devastate a specific area, but spread little fallout beyond the target. The efforts in this direction have to a certain extent succeeded.

Over the years there has been a great deal of talk about radioactive fallout, but in fact we know frighteningly little about its long-range effects on human life. There is so much uncertainty that predicted effects are usually heavily influenced by the social or political outlook of the expert making the prediction. Scientists and technicians who are opposed to war issue gloomy predictions.

All but the most glowingly optimistic predictions about the world after a thermonuclear war agree that while there might be survivors of such a war there would be no "winners." No nation would be better off or more powerful than before the war began. The general consensus is that thermonuclear war would be an irrational and insane act. But most wars seem irrational and insane, yet the history of man is the history of almost constant war.

Recently it has become fashionable to think of man as being "innately aggressive." Some biologists and students of animal behavior have advanced the theory that, for a variety of evolutionary reasons, man has become a "natural killer" who is often unable to use his rational mind to stop killing.

If men feel that their "homeland" or "territory" is threatened by an enemy they might launch a nuclear war. Such a war would destroy the territory of both the "enemy" and the "defender," but there would be no stopping it, because the reaction to fight would be "instinctive."

In his highly popular book *The Naked Ape* zoologist Desmond Morris states the problem this way: "Unhappily where matters as basic as territorial defense are concerned, our higher brain centers are all too susceptible to the urgings of our lower ones. Intellectual control can help us just so far, but no further. In the last resort it is unreliable, and a single unreasoned, emotional act can undo all the good it has achieved."

In short, some scientists think that man is simply too irrational, too aggressive, and too blindly emotional to be trusted with weapons that could bring about his own destruction. But the weapons are already here. Some controls may be placed on nuclear weapons in the future. The unlimited testing of nuclear weapons has already been halted, largely because of the danger of fallout from such tests. But the weapons are not going to go away. We must simply hope that man can act rationally enough to avoid the suicidal folly of deliberate nuclear war.

There is always the possibility of a major war starting accidentally. The various warning systems and missile systems are highly automated, and we are assured by those who control these systems that a catastrophic mistake is "impossible." But in the face of such assurances one is always reminded of the fate of the "unsinkable" *Titanic,* which sank on its maiden voyage.

Then there is the thought that some nation might decide on the ultimate weapon, the Doomsday Machine.

The Doomsday Machine is a name that is given to any weapon that is specifically designed to destroy the entire world. Obviously, any nation that built such a weapon would hope that it would never be used. But the Doomsday Machine is not merely some comic-book mad scientist's dream. The power of the Doomsday Machine would be its threat. It would be the perfect instrument of blackmail. The whole world would be held hostage, like the passengers and crew of an airliner that has been hijacked by a man who claims to have a bomb strapped to his chest. If the hijacker's demands are not met, he says he will blow up the plane, killing himself but everybody else as well. Perhaps he wouldn't really set off the bomb in the end, perhaps he doesn't even have a bomb, or the bomb might malfunction when he pressed the button. But who would care to take the chance? A nation possessing the Doomsday Machine might say, "Meet our demands or we will blow up the world."

Could a Doomsday Machine actually be built? The answer, unfortunately, is yes. There are several approaches which might be taken. The most practical in terms of current weapons technology would be a cobalt bomb, or more probably a series of cobalt bombs. The cobalt bomb would be an ordinary atomic bomb encased in a jacket of cobalt. Such a bomb would be extremely "dirty," that is, when it exploded it would spread a tremendous amount of radioactive fallout throughout the world. If enough cobalt bombs were exploded they could seriously endanger the continued existence of life on this planet.

What makes such a weapon dangerously attractive is that it would be a lot cheaper and easier to build than the elaborate nuclear missile systems now possessed by the U.S. and the U.S.S.R. The Doomsday Machine would be a quick way for a second-line power to attain great-power status.

Another type of Doomsday Machine that has been discussed would work by placing large hydrogen bombs at certain strategic spots on earth and then exploding them simultaneously. This might cause the earth to wobble on its axis and bring about heaven knows what worldwide catastrophes. A variation of this idea would be to spot hydrogen bombs along major fault lines and set them off in the hopes of triggering a worldwide series of disastrous earthquakes. Such suggestions are probably impractical (they are undoubtedly insane, of course) and belong more within the realm of science fiction.

Definitely within the realm of awful possibility is the "asteroid bomb" first suggested about a decade ago by the late Dandridge Cole, a professional speculator for the General Electric Corporation. Cole postulated that by the 1980s we might be able to capture one of the large asteroids in the asteroid belt. By firing thousands of megatons worth of nuclear bombs at the right point the asteroid could be directed into an orbit around the earth. There it would hover until the moment that those who controlled it pressed the button that would fire the rockets that would send the asteroid crashing into the earth. We have already discussed what the impact of a really large asteroid might do to us.

War, the rider on the red horse, is now more than a symbol of the apocalypse.

Famine, the rider on the black horse, has also taken on a ghastly new meaning in the modern world. In biblical times famines occurred regularly, and they were to be feared. At that time, any bad harvest might bring about mass starvation. In most places there was little or no reserve food. But over the centuries as civilization advanced it seemed as though the problem of famine might be finally overcome.

Then in 1798 a pessimistic English curate named Thomas Robert Malthus wrote a highly influential work called *An Essay on the Principle of Population.* "The power of population is indefinately greater than the power in the earth to produce subsistence for man," Malthus said.

"Population when unchecked, increases in a geometrical ratio. Subsistence increases only in an arithmetical ratio. A slight acquaintance with numbers will show the immensity of the first power in comparison of the second."

Malthus believed that lack of food—starvation—would provide the ultimate check on the growth of human population. "By that law of our nature which makes food necessary to the life of a man, the effects of these two unequal powers must be kept equal.

"This implies a strong and constantly operating check on population from the difficulty of subsistence."

For a while, Malthus's ideas were very widely believed. But as agricultural technology advanced more rapidly than Malthus or anyone else of his time could have foreseen it looked as though he might be proved wrong. Much more food was being produced on less land by fewer workers. A vastly increased population could be fed. From the time Malthus wrote to the present day the world's population has increased from one billion to three billion.

But in the long run Malthus was right, as we now realize. Technology and improved farming methods have been able to feed the increased population. But people are still not being fed very well. Most of the world's people are undernourished as they always have been. In many nations the benefits of improvements in agricultural technology have been wiped out by a population that increases faster than the food supply. As you read this sentence four people will have died from starvation. Most of them will be children.

There are a few bright spots. In some parts of Asia the introduction of new high-yield seeds and improved farming methods have produced a food surplus for the first time in history even though the population has multiplied. But such improvements simply delay the inevitable. The dilemma first described by Malthus will not disappear.

Mass famines are still very much a part of the modern world. As these words are being written hundreds of thousands of refugees from a war in Bangladesh (formerly East Pakistan) face starvation despite a worldwide relief effort. A few months ago it was the victims of a war in Nigeria who were starving. A few months from now it may be the people of India or Indonesia who are under the shadow of the rider on the black horse. Population experts warn that famines will continue to increase during the decade of the 1970s and that hundreds of millions of people will die, and there is nothing at all that can be done about it.

Clearly, unless the world's population is limited, and limited drastically, the future is not going to be very nice to contemplate. But it is possible that the unchecked growth of population might actually bring about the end of the world? We will not squeeze one another to death or breathe up all the air, but a vastly increased population could certainly help bring about the end of the world in a number of ways.

The Population Division of the United Nations has tentatively estimated that 15 billion people is the absolute upper limit that the earth can sustain. The current world population is about three billion. If present trends are not reversed the world's population is increasing so rapidly that it will reach that 15 billion limit in only two centuries. The world's population will double within the next thirty-five years, and after that the increase will be even more rapid.

We are undergoing what is called a population explosion. Population explosions are not limited to *Homo sapiens*. Many species of animals, mice, rats, lemmings, and even deer experience occasional population explosions. No matter what we may think of our own mental and spiritual qualities, biologically we are just another species of animal. We would be blind to think that we could escape the laws which control other species.

In the animal world a species may go along for many years with a stable population. Then some new factor, perhaps the introduction of a new source of food or the disappearance of an effective predator, allows the species to expand dramatically within a short time. But the explosive population growth can not and does not continue indefinitely. It is followed by an even more dramatic and rapid population collapse.

Scientists who have studied the mechanics of population explosions and collapses in the laboratory and in the field have made a number of interesting and quite terrifying observations. First, a vastly expanded population of any single species will eventually eat itself out of its own food supply.

The animals also crowd themselves out of suitable living areas. Many individuals thus have no place to raise their young or to hide from potential predators.

But usually before such extreme conditions are reached nature puts other mechanisms into operation to bring down the swollen population. Under very crowded conditions many animals seem to go mad. Normally nonaggressive animals will begin to fight ferociously. Females lose the ability or the desire to care for their young and the infant mortality rate rises sharply. Animals begin pointless and usually fatal migrations.

The migrating lemmings that jump into the sea are the best-known example of this sort of apparently suicidal mass movement. The lemmings are not driven to migrate solely by hunger. Lemmings often desert areas in which the food supply is still abundant after their population rises above a certain level. It is crowding not starvation that drives them.

In swollen populations the individual's resistance to disease appears to go down. Finally many apparently healthy animals just drop dead for no obvious reason. The cause seems to be some sort of hormonal change in the body, but we are not sure how or why this comes about.

Translated into human terms what does all of this mean? It means famine, war, epidemics, increased personal violence, and the sort of general breakdown in social structure that many believe we are now beginning to experience.

We talked briefly about the possibility that man possesses an innately aggressive nature. If this indeed is true, then population increase is the worst thing that could possibly happen to our species. The more we press in on one another, the more we activate one another's aggressive drives and the greater the possibility of war, even suicidal thermonuclear war.

Dr. Paul R. Ehrlich, professor of biology at Stanford

University and one of the leading spokesmen for population control, has envisioned a number of possible futures that might come about if the human population continues to grow as rapidly as it has been. One would be a thermonuclear war that would take place about 1979. Here is how Dr. Ehrlich describes the end of this war:

"The effects include rising radiation levels and climatic catastrophe resulting from the addition of enormous amounts of debris and carbon dioxide to the atmosphere. These and general sterilization of the soil (followed by massive erosion) make the northern two-thirds of the Earth uninhabitable. Pollution of the sea is vastly increased. Small pockets of *Homo sapiens* hold on for a while in the Southern Hemisphere, but slowly die out as social systems break down, radiation poisoning takes effect, climatic changes kill crops, livestock dies off, and various man-made plagues spread. The most intelligent creatures ultimately surviving this period are cockroaches."

But as Dr. Ehrlich is quick to point out, this grisly future is only a possibility of what might happen, not a prediction of what will happen.

The rider on the pale horse, death in the form of plague or other epidemic disease, has also taken on a new meaning in today's world. There had of course been "plagues" that we call epidemics since the dawn of history. But like famines and wars they were looked upon only as possible signs of the coming end.

Perhaps the worst epidemic ever to hit the Western World was the Black Death (probably an epidemic of bubonic or black plague) that raged through Europe in the Middle Ages. The Black Death ultimately killed off an estimated one fourth to one third of the population of Europe. It significantly set back the progress of European civilization.

During the plague years there were numerous end-of-the-world panics. People did not understand the reasons for the plague. The Black Death was thought to be divine punishment for their wickedness. In plague-torn Europe Judgment Day itself seemed very close at hand.

Deadly worldwide epidemics are not a thing of the dim past, nor do they strike only the poor and backward nations. In 1918 an influenza epidemic killed half a million persons in the United States and twenty million throughout the world.

Diseases can be particularly disastrous when they are introduced among a population that has had no previous contact with them and thus has developed no immunities. Smallpox had been a scourge in Europe for centuries. Many died of it every year. But many also survived the disease (and thus were immune to it for life) while others simply never got it.

The effects of this disease were far more catastrophic when it was introduced among the American Indians and the peoples of the South Pacific Islands. Though both of these peoples were exceptionally healthy, far healthier than the average European of the day, they were helpless in the face of new diseases. Whole tribes of Indians were wiped out in smallpox epidemics. On isolated Easter Island a smallpox epidemic in 1866 reduced the population from several thousand to a few hundred. In the end the white man's diseases probably did more damage than the white man's guns.

It was this real fear of encountering some sort of new disease against which we would have no resistance, which led to the practice of quarantining the first few astronauts who had been on the moon. Scientists were almost dead sure that the moon was biologically sterile, that it could not contain any germs. But the costly and time-consuming quarantine practice was continued through two flights just to make absolutely sure. Diseases from other worlds will be a constant concern if and when man begins to explore other planets.

Yet another fear is artificially created germs that could be so virulent that there would be no protection against them. From time to time there is talk of how effective biological warfare would be. Theoretically "supergerms" can be created in the laboratory. The military problem is that any country that launched an attack with such potent germs would also fall victim to them. This raises the possibility of a biological Doomsday Machine.

Just how far along the road to creating such powerful germs we have already gone it is impossible to say. Much research in biological warfare had been conducted by the major powers of the world. But the results of this research remain a closely guarded secret. At this moment all the major powers have agreed to give up biological-weapons research and destroy existing stocks of biological weapons. However, as long as the technology to produce such weapons exists the temptation to use them will remain.

What is even more frightening is that it would not take a major power to create a devastating stock of biological weapons. Dr. Brock Chisholm of Canada who has studied the subject extensively pointed out that any country, or for that matter any sizable group that includes a good biologist and a few appropriately experienced technicians who had worked in penicillin or other biological production could produce sufficient biological weapons to launch a large-scale attack on the United States.

This conjures up the vision of some supersecret organization of evil men suddenly presenting all the nations of the world with an ultimatum, "Pay us billions of dollars or we will release our supergerms and destroy the world."

Science-fiction writers have used this sort of idea exten-

sively. But happily, destroying the world would not be quite
as simple a job as it is made to seem in stories. A few ounces
of the toxin or poison produced by the botulis bacteria,
would be deadly enough to kill the entire world and such
toxin is easy to produce.

But how could the poison be administered? It would
have to be sprayed over all populated areas. This would be
difficult, to say the least. The theoretical group of evildoers
could not work cheaply or in secrecy. Anybody buying up
large numbers of airplanes or privately building long-range
missiles is bound to be noticed.

Toxins are poisons. They have to be encountered directly
to do any harm. Living disease germs, however, are infec-
tious. Germs could be released in one place, and the disease
they produce would spread throughout the world. No elaborate delivery systems would be needed. But even the most
virulent diseases spread fairly slowly. Before such a plague
got anywhere near destroying the world a defense against it
might be found. The spread of the disease might also be kept
in check by normal quarantine procedures.

A real doomsday biological attack would almost certainly
have to be launched by a major power using its planes and
missiles to deliver massive quantities of germs over broad
areas of the world. The disease would then spread so quickly
there would be no chance of stopping it. Since major powers
already rely on nuclear weapons it seems highly unlikely
they would switch their weapons of destruction at this late
date. The biological Doomsday Machine is more of a night-
mare than a real possibility.

Recently mankind has become increasingly alarmed that
the end of the world might be brought about by a new kind
of man-made plague—pollution. We are currently poisoning
our air and water at a horrifying rate. As the population

Two photographs showing the explosion of an underwater atomic bomb at Bikini atoll in the Pacific in July 1946. *Joint Task Force One*

rises the needs for fresh air and fresh water also rises. So too do the demands for power and manufactured goods which produce the pollution in the first place. Something has to give.

There are many things which can be done to cut down on pollution right now. But mankind tends to react slowly and reluctantly, even in the face of a grave crisis. The dangers of the long-lived pesticide DDT were well-known for years before any action to ban the use of this chemical was taken. It is hard for people to give up short-term benefits because of long-term dangers.

No amount of pollution control, no matter how effective, is going to do much good without population control. If the population growth continues unchecked it may be pollution poisoning of one sort or another, rather than starvation which will kill off the greatest number of people.

There is no doubt that unless we radically reverse some of the trends of modern life, namely unrestricted population growth and virtually unrestricted technology the future is going to be crowded, dirty and generally unpleasant. Fortunately the seriousness of the problems have at least been recognized, and a small start toward reversing the slide toward environmental disaster has been made. Much has been written in recent years about the problems of pollution, and general environmental damage, but our subject here is not the quality of life in the future, but the very existence of life.

In his poem "The Hollow Men," T. S. Eliot wrote, "This is the way the world ends, Not with a bang but a whimper." Eliot's ominous statement has been repeated often by those concerned about the destruction of our environment. Mankind seems to be strangling in his own waste products. This, say the environmentalists, is the whimper with which the world might end.

Dr. Paul Ehrlich has outlined some of the possible doomsday effects of massive pollution:

"Man's activities and construction also have significant local effects on weather, but it is his influence on large scale climatic change that is of greatest concern, for there can be little doubt that such change has been accelerated on a global basis with almost complete disregard for possible consequences. Some of the changes which have been predicted would be cataclysmic—slippage of the Antarctic ice cap, causing tidal waves which would wipe out most of humanity; or the sudden onset of a new ice age. But even in the absence of such extreme (and hopefully remote!) possibilities, the results of rapid climatic change would be lethal both for many humans and for many other organisms."

When the U.S. Congress was debating the desirability of funding the supersonic transport or SST, there was some talk that the planes could create a "global gloom." Dr. V.J. Schaefer, an atmospheric physicist and director of the Atmospheric Sciences Research Center at Albany, N.Y., was one of the first to give widespread publicity to this idea. He worried out loud that a fleet of SSTs discharging some 150,-000 tons of water vapor every day from fuel combustion might create a permanent cloud in the upper atmosphere.

A scene from the movie Dr. Strangelove. In this black comedy about an accidental American nuclear attack on the Soviet Union Peter Sellers (right) as the President is on the hot line trying to persuade the Soviet Premier not to retaliate with the Doomsday Machine. *Culver Pictures*

The result would be "global gloom," a general blockage of sunlight throughout the world. A committee set up by the President of the United States also mentioned the possibility that the SST could raise the humidity of the upper atmosphere and "alter the radiation balance and thereby possibly affect the general circulation of atmospheric components."

Wisely, Congress rejected the funds to build a U.S. SST. Other nations, however, have gone ahead with the project.

The general pollution of the atmosphere might lower the temperature of the earth by blocking sunlight, or it might raise the temperature of the earth by what is known as the greenhouse effect. Normally the sun's radiation passes through the atmosphere, and a certain percentage of it is reflected back into space. But a badly polluted atmosphere might trap a higher percentage of the radiation and reflect it back to earth thus raising the average temperature. The long-range effects of either raising or lowering the average temperature of the earth are unknown.

We might also radiate ourselves out of existence even without a nuclear war. An increased population demands increased power, and we are fast running out of coal, oil, and natural gas. Besides, burning these fuels pollutes the atmosphere. The future power needs of mankind are supposed to be filled by nuclear reactors. But opponents of nuclear power warn that the radioactive wastes from the reactors will be difficult and dangerous to dispose of and that even the best-constructed nuclear plants will release a little low-level radioactivity into the atmosphere. The widespread use of nuclear reactors will almost certainly raise the level of background radiation on the earth. What effect will this have on human life? We really can't say, because we just don't know.

The rising worldwide levels of other potentially dangerous pollutants like mercury and lead may also have disastrous consequences for our species.

With all of these dangers, however, only a very few predict the outright end of the world through pollution or any human activity short of thermonuclear war. Whether life in an overcrowded and badly polluted world will be worth living is quite another matter.

CHAPTER 8

The Earth Itself

Day after day, more people come to L.A. Shhh, don't you tell anybody the whole place is slipping away. Where can we go, when there's no San Francisco? Better get ready to tie up the boat in Idaho. Do you know the swim? You better learn quick, Jim. Those who don't know the swim, better sing the hymn.

—From "Day after Day."
© 1969 Irving Music Inc.
Goombay Music (BMI)

The closest thing to a genuine end-of-the-world panic to hit the United States in recent years centered in the state of California in 1968 and 1969. Some of the reasons for this fear, the predicted rising of Atlantis and the close approach of the asteroid Icarus, have been discussed in previous chapters. But the principal emotion behind the California scare was man's attitude toward earthquakes.

Says Charles F. Richter, Professor of seismology at the California Institute of Technology, "Earthquakes, pestilence,

187

famine. From time immemorial these were thought to be direct manifestations of the displeasure of offended powers, while eclipses and comets were regarded as their terrible precursors. But with the growth of urban civilization and the improvement in communications, such superstitions are gradually disappearing. . . .

"Only earthquakes remain largely misunderstood, the object of unreasoning fear. A sudden catastrophe, with tens, even hundreds of thousands of lives lost in a single event, naturally excites the apprehensive imagination. . . ."

As Dr. Richter points out, earthquakes are not only feared for their destructive potential, which is enormous, but because they are looked upon as a sign of divine punishment. Indeed the Bible mentions "great earthquakes" as one of the signs foretelling the end of the world. "And I beheld when he had opened the sixth seal, and, lo, there was a great earthquake; and the sun became black as sackcloth of hair, and the moon became as blood." (Revelation 6:12) Certainly the fears and rumors of destruction that circulated throughout California in 1968 and 1969 combined all the traditional elements of an end-of-the-world panic.

Of course, people in California are quite right to fear earthquakes. Ninety percent of all the recorded earthquakes in the United States occur in California. Thousands of earthquakes of varying intensity strike California each year. The vast majority of these quakes do no damage. Most are noticed only by seismologists checking their sensitive earthquake-detecting instruments. Only about 1 in 10,000 earthquakes causes any damage at all in the state. But occasionally California has been subjected to disastrous earthquakes, in which many died and there was tremendous damage.

Prior to the 1968–69 scare, the last great earthquake to

strike the state was in 1906. That was the famous San Francisco earthquake which resulted in the devastation of a large part of that city. Some seven hundred people died, mostly from the fire which followed the quake. California real-estate developers don't like to talk about earthquakes, which are bad for business. They prefer to call the event the San Francisco fire.

The San Francisco quake, bad as it was, is by no means the most destructive earthquake on record. Some 10,000 persons died as the result of an earthquake in Chile in 1960 (the strongest quake ever recorded). The famous Lisbon earthquake of 1755 killed 60,000. The most deadly of all earthquakes was one which struck Shensi Province in Central China in 1556. Then an estimated 830,000 persons died.

Most large quakes occur along what are called faults. The immediate cause of the 1906 quake was the San Andreas Fault, an ominous-looking six-hundred-mile-long crack in the surface of the earth from Mendocino to the Gulf of California. Normally one side of a fault moves slowly, vertically or horizontally in relation to the other. But sometimes this slow movement does not take place, or does not take place rapidly enough to relieve the forces building up beneath the ground. Then stress develops along the fault and when a readjustment of the two sides of the fault does finally take place it is rapid and violent. It is an earthquake.

There had been a major earthquake along the San Andreas Fault in 1857. The next one was the quake of 1906, an interval of forty-nine years. Since 1906 there have been no major earthquakes in California. Thus the stresses along the fault had been building for over sixty years. A major earthquake seemed overdue.

Seismologists and geologists generally do not like to scare people with tales of imminent earthquakes. Time and again

The destruction caused by the San Francisco earthquake and accompanying fire of 1906 was awesome, though the quake itself was by no means the most powerful or most destructive on record. *The Library of Congress*

they stress that there is no way of telling when or exactly where a major earthquake will strike. But the scientists too were a bit worried about the San Andreas Fault and some of this worry spilled over to the general public and helped increase the growing "earthquake fever."

In 1968 Dr. Richter stated that in California "every community is within striking distance of one or more of the important faults." With uncharacteristic bluntness he added, "We must expect repetitions of the great earthquakes of 1906 and 1857." In 1969 Dr. William T. Pecora, director of the U.S. Geological Survey, testified before a congressional committee that California was in a "steady state of restlessness." He predicted "another massive earthquake, certainly within the next 30 years and probably within the next decade." In a popular book called *Earthquake Country* Robert Iacopi wrote: "California's next great earthquake may take place while you are reading this book, or it may not come during our lifetime. But one thing is sure: it is definitely on the way." These were the sober and responsible opinions, and they scared people.

Astrologers, mystic prophets, and assorted crackpots vied with one another for picking the exact date for doomsday in California. A San Francisco woman got a lot of publicity when she placed her hand over a map of California and said that she felt "bad vibrations" from the Fresno area. This she said meant that there would be a major earthquake in April 1968. She and her family then left the state.

April was a favored month for earthquake prophets. The last major earthquake in the U.S. had taken place in Alaska on Good Friday of 1964. In 1968 Good Friday came in April. Besides the 1906 quake had also taken place in April. That sort of dating doesn't make much sense, but mystic earthquake prophecy rarely makes much sense.

One group of earthquake predictors led by someone calling himself Arch Druid Morloch advanced a plan to move great works of art out of the state by teleportation. But the Arch Druid and his followers said they would stick around to study the earthquake "as an art form."

A minor sensation was created by a book, published in 1968, called *The Last Days of the Late Great State of California*. The author was Curt Gentry, a California journalist. The book was primarily an angry comment on the politics and life-style of modern Californians. But that is not what made it a sensation. California life has been criticized before. What people really wanted to read was the author's highly realistic and dramatic description of a gigantic earthquake that supposedly destroyed most of the state in 1969.

"It came out of the Pacific at the mouth of Alder creek by Point Arena—just as on April 18, 1906, only this time much stronger—ripped south at the steady, crunching speed of two miles per second, causing the Garcia and Gualala rivers to jump their banks, splitting giant trees right down the middle, then passing directly under the small town of Plantation.

"First killed was a painter catapulted from a house roof, next 8 students departing from their last class at Fort Ross School.

"It continued south, within a mile of the old Russian trading post, snapping the historic buildings like matchsticks, trapping 9 in the debris, nosing underwater again, to resurface at Bodega Head.

"At this moment buildings were toppling in Santa Rosa, Petaluma, Napa, and even Sacramento—a full 75 miles east of the San Andreas Fault. At Oroville, 150 miles away, ominous cracks appeared in the dam.

"It split south through the waters of Tomales Bay, cap-

There had been numerous predictions of a major earthquake in California in 1968 or 1969. It didn't happen. But there was a good sized earthquake there in February of 1971. Among other things, the quake collapsed this freeway overpass in the San Fernando Valley. *U.S. Geological Survey*

sizing small craft and drowning 12 before passing under Olema and Bolinas to return to the ocean."

But this was only the beginning. Somewhat later a news broadcaster receiving reports on the disaster suddenly exclaims:

"Oh, My God! Los Angeles has vanished! Planes have explored the whole basin, and out of all of the vast region known as Los Angeles County only two cities in the northeast portion—Palmdale and Lancaster—remain.

"This is—"

"Wait a minute. There's more. Orange County is gone too. And most of San Diego. And . . ."

All California west of the San Andreas Fault was supposed to have fallen into the ocean.

The book did not reveal an exact date for the future disaster, just that it was supposed to have occurred at 3:13

on a Friday afternoon in 1969. During the height of the
scare *The Last Days of the Late Great State of California*
and practically any other book that had to do with earthquakes became instant best-sellers in California.

The scientific community was enraged by all this fuss.
Scientists at the California Institute of Technology released
a strong statement about the earthquake prophecies: "Wild
predictions of disastrous earthquakes—issued by self-pro-
claimed oracles and other visionaries—are not supported by
scientific evidence and are frightening many Californians
needlessly."

The majority of Californians probably did not take these
earthquake prophecies too seriously, though most may have
worried a bit more about the danger of earthquakes during
1968 and 1969 than they normally did. Certainly everybody
was talking about earthquakes. Some people, however, actually left the state. Among those who fled were some apoca-
lyptic-minded ministers and their congregations who believed
that California was a sinful state and was going to be destroyed because it deserved to be destroyed.

The scare inevitably spawned its own brand of black
humor. A man named Greg Chursenoff of Van Nuys wrote
to a newspaper: "It is true that a disastrous earthquake will
split California at the San Andreas Fault. However, there is
no reason for alarm because it is the Eastern section of the
United States that will sink into the ocean."

During 1968 and 1969, predicted doomsday followed predicted doomsday and nothing special happened. There were
earthquakes, of course, but there always are earthquakes in
California. There were no major quakes during the fateful
two years. People got bored with the whole subject and the
prophets of doom began putting off the date of the great
quake to the end of the century.

When another major quake finally did strike the state it was in February of 1971, a time that none of the soothsayers or prophets had predicted. Nor was this quake triggered by the feared San Andreas Fault. The villain was a smaller fault nearby. In the 1971 quake some sixty persons were killed and the value of property damaged reached an estimated billion dollars. It was a disaster of major proportions, but it was a far cry from the state shattering catastrophe that had been so widely predicted.

On the whole relationship of earthquakes to end-of-the-world hysteria Dr. Richter has written:

"One notices with some amusement that certain religious groups have picked this rather unfortunate time to insist that the number of earthquakes is increasing. In part they are misled by the increasing number of small earthquakes that are being cataloged and listed by newer, more sensitive [seismological] stations throughout the world. It is worth remarking that the number of great earthquakes from 1896 to 1906 (about twenty-five) was greater than in any ten-year interval since.

"Apparently this religious concern is associated with some of the words of the Gospels referring to the last days: 'and there shall be famines and pestilences and earthquakes, in divers places.' Assuredly, no safer forecast was ever made. One of the evangelists, or perhaps a copyist, added emphasis by reading 'great earthquakes'; that still impresses a seismologist as not much of a prediction."

But could it happen, could the earth literally be shaken apart by a series of gigantic earthquakes? The answer is a slightly qualified no. Slightly qualified because no one really knows what causes earthquakes in the first place, nor what the quakes themselves do to the earth.

It is easy enough to say that the vast majority of earthquakes are caused by strains deep within the earth—but what causes these strains? There is a relatively new theory that has gained wide acceptance. Over the last two decades ocean-ographers have discovered that there is a worldwide network of cracks or fractures that bisect most of the great ocean basins. There is some evidence to indicate that molten ma-terial welling up from the mantle beneath the earth's solid crust is forced out through these midocean cracks. The con-stant pressure of this upward welling material actually causes the sea floor to spread.

As the sea floor is pushed toward the continents it is blocked in some places. There the solid sea-floor material is forced downward, under the continents and deep into the molten mantle of the earth. In the Pacific, as the spreading sea floor approaches surrounding islands or mountain arcs, such as the Aleutian Islands, Japan, the Tonga Islands, or western South America, crustal material is forced downward. The stresses caused by the downward push of the crustal material results in earthquakes and increasing volcanic ac-tivity.

But since sea-floor spreading goes on all of the time this theory does not get at the basic cause of earthquakes. It only explains why earthquakes are common in certain areas not why they occur when they do. An even newer theory links sea-floor spreading, and hence earthquakes, to slight wobbles in the earth's rotation. That the earth wobbles slightly on its axis has been known for more than eighty years. At one time it was suggested that this slight wobble might be caused by the disruptive effects of earthquakes. But at the time scientists thought that the effects of earth-quakes, however great locally, were just that—local. The worldwide effect of a single earthquake, even a major one, did not seem great enough to wobble the whole earth.

However, with the development of more sensitive equipment scientists have discovered that the worldwide effects of earthquakes is much greater than previously believed. Great enough, according to two assistant professors of the department of geophysics at the University of Western Ontario in Canada, to throw the planet's axis slightly askew. The geophysicists L. Mansinha and D. E. Smylie reported their theory in the *Journal of Geophysical Research* in 1967. In 1968 the two Canadians refined their research. They found that during the years 1957 to 1968 there were forty-one wobbles in the earth's rotation. Mansinha and Smylie believe they are able to relate thirty-two of the forty-one wobbles to the occurrence of major earthquakes.

This idea was taken up by Dr. James R. Heirtzler of Columbia University, one of the pioneers of the concept of sea-floor spreading. Every few months, according to his hypothesis, "there are changes in the earth's rotational motion that affect sea floor spreading and cause the earthquakes associated with it. If such a change is large enough it may even reverse the earth's magnetic field."

According to Dr. Heirtzler, "rather minor variations" of the earth's rotation axis "can affect to a surprising extent both the climate at the surface of the earth and forces and stresses within the earth."

Further, Dr. Heirtzler has pointed out that some scientists have speculated on some sort of a relationship between the reversals of the earth's magnetic field and episodes of active mountain building. This would make the wobbles in the earth's spin even more important.

In Chapter 6 we already discussed the possible relationship between episodes of magnetic reversals and the large-scale extinction of species.

Dr. Heirtzler admits that his entire hypothesis is highly

The most violent recorded earthquake in the U.S. hit Alaska on Good Friday (March 27) 1964. Buildings in Anchorage crumbled like matchsticks. *American Red Cross*

The Good Friday Earthquake not only tore down buildings it displaced the earth's surface over an area of more than 100,000 square miles. Photo shows the dramatic uplift of land the Hanning Bay Fault scarp, on Montague Island. *U.S. Geological Survey*

speculative. But he believes that it explains better than any
other theory currently available many of the new things
that we are discovering about the earth.

In this theory, earthquakes are a minor by-product of
the earth's wobble and not the sort of activity that would in
any way bring about the end of the world. Even if we held
that earthquakes are the cause of the earth's wobble, they
might bring about the end of the world only in the most
indirect way. Certainly there is nothing currently known
about earthquakes, nor anything on the farthest fringes of
responsible scientific speculation, that gives earthquakes the
doomsday powers often attributed to them.

During the height of the California earthquake scare a
popular item was a large gold, black, and orange poster
showing the city of San Francisco careening into the sea.
The snappy calypso song about the disaster quoted at the
beginning of this chapter gives the same picture.

Practically everybody who believed that there was going
to be a great earthquake as predicted had some sort of idea
that part of the state was going to break off and sink into
the ocean. Such a belief implies that continents either are
like boats, floating on top of the ocean, or are shaped like
mushrooms with their coastlines protruding over the water
or perhaps are hollow and could collapse under their own
weight.

But in truth, continents are quite solid, right down
through the earth's crust. Most coastlines do not hang out
over the ocean. In fact most are surrounded by a continental
shelf, which slopes gently downward under water till it
meets the ocean floor.

Earthquakes can cause a general subsiding of large parts
of a continent, and this may drown limited coastal areas. In
the May 1960 earthquake that struck Chile some five thou-

sand square miles dropped about six feet. This came as quite a shock to many geologists who didn't think that earthquakes could have such a catastrophic effect. But this still did not result in major portions of Chile dropping into the sea. The Good Friday earthquake in Alaska altered the Alaskan coastline slightly, but Anchorage, a port city, did not disappear beneath the waves. So no matter how great an earthquake occurs, no large portions of California, or any other coastal area for that matter, are going to break off and fall, slip, slide, or otherwise descend into the ocean.

Often one hears that coastal areas are devastated by water after a quake, but this flooding is a side effect of the quake. Alaska's Good Friday earthquake created tidal waves, or *tsunamis,* which struck all along the West Coast. These huge waves did swamp many low-lying areas from Alaska to California and were ultimately far more destructive than the direct effects of the quake itself. Most tidal waves are created by undersea earthquakes. The quake did not—repeat, not—sink any major portions of land under the sea.

So the rapid sinking of continents (like Atlantis) is simply fantasy.

Volcanoes are if anything even more spectacular examples of the terrifying power of nature. Yet they have never been notably connected with end-of-the-world fears, except for people who lived on volcanic islands. There are two reasons why volcanoes don't inspire the same sort of apocalyptic visions that earthquakes do. Most of our subconscious feelings and fears about the end of the world are drawn from the Bible, and ultimately from the mythology of the ancient Middle East. The Middle East is an area which contains few active volcanoes, so men would not have worried much about them.

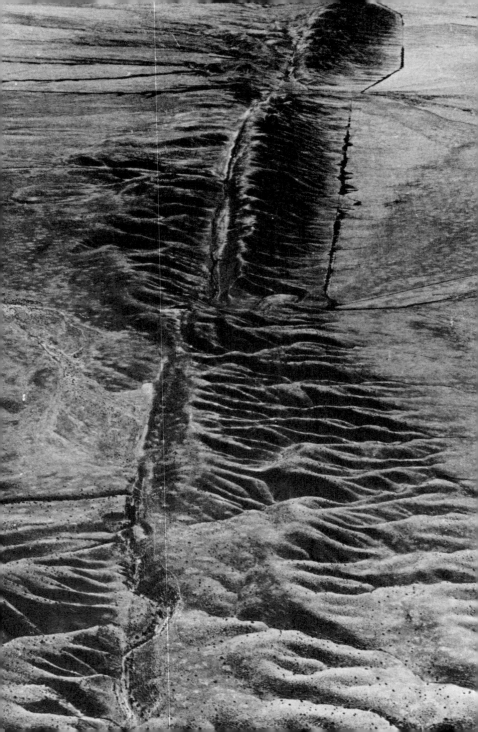

RECENT EARTH MOVE-
MENTS ALONG FAULT
HAVE DISPLACED
STREAM CHANNEL
FROM A TO B

REPEATED MOVEMENTS
OVER THOUSANDS OF
YEARS HAVE DISPLACED
CHANNEL FROM A TO C

B

C

500 FEET

A

SAN ANDREAS
FAULT

An aerial view of the notorious San Andreas fault in the Carrizo Plain area of central California. *U.S. Geological Survey*

Aerial view of the Carrizo Plain area, in Central California showing displacements of stream channels caused by earth movements along the San Andreas Fault. *U.S. Geological Survey*

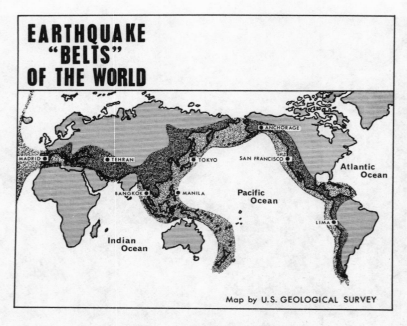

EARTHQUAKE "BELTS" OF THE WORLD

Map by U.S. GEOLOGICAL SURVEY

Earthquake "Belts" of the World.

But in volcanic areas volcanoes did become part of the end-of-the-world mythology. You may recall that in the discussion of the Norse Ragnarök (Chapter 2) it is the fire giant Surt who sets the world aflame after the final battle. Surt is clearly a mythological creature of the volcano. Our knowledge of Norse mythology comes largely from the Eddas, Icelandic poems, and Iceland is a volcanic island.

Mount Hekla, Iceland's most active volcano, has often erupted violently and dangerously during the historical times. Christians thought that by looking into Hekla's craters one could see the main entrance to hell. A twelfth-century monk, after describing an eruption of the volcano proclaimed, "Who now is there so refractory and unbelieving that he will not credit the existence of eternal fire where souls suffer, when with his own eyes he sees the fire of which I have spoke." Until recently when one Swede wanted to tell another to "go to hell" he told him to "go to Hekla."

Unlike an earthquake which strikes without warning, volcanic explosions are seldom unexpected. Volcanoes usually smoke and bubble for days or weeks before a major explosion takes place. Sometimes volcanic explosions have been responsible for appalling losses of human life, but this was not because of the suddenness or violence of the eruption, but because people did not, or could not, heed the warnings. In 1902 some forty thousand people died as the result of an eruption of Mount Pelée on Martinique in the Caribbean. But the tragedy was an entirely unnecessary one. There had been plenty of warning that the volcano was about to erupt violently. Yet no attempt was made to evacuate the residents of the nearby town of St. Pierre. The negligence and downright stupidity of the authorities of Martinique prepared the way for one of the world's great tragedies. Not only did the authorities fail to encourage people living in St. Pierre to leave, until the violence subsided, they actually tried to prevent them from leaving. First the authorities published a flock of misleading statements assuring everyone that everything would be all right if they just remained calm. But the activity of the volcano became even more ominous and many attempted to flee anyway. The authorities actually set up roadblocks, and thousands were trapped when the main eruption took place. The disaster of Mount Pelée is more of an indictment of man than of the violence of nature.

An even greater volcanic eruption took place in 1883 on the small island of Krakatoa in what is now the nation of Indonesia. After belching out smoke and ash for months, the volcano on Krakatoa literally blew apart on the morning of

April 27. Krakatoa exploded four times in succession. The explosion that took place at 10:02 A.M. was the loudest explosion in recorded history. As far away as Rodriguez Island in the Indian Ocean, nearly three thousand miles from Krakatoa, people heard the blast and said it sounded like, "the distant roar of heavy guns."

The island itself had rested upon a huge underground cavern filled with molten rock. When the major eruptions took place this cavern was emptied out. As a result a large part of the island sank into the sea. Places that had been a thousand feet above the water were suddenly plunged a thousand feet below. In Chapter 2 we discussed the ancient explosion of the volcano Santorini and its possible relationship to the legend of Atlantis. Very much the same sort of thing that happened at Krakatoa must have taken place at Santorini thirty-five hundred years ago. Large portions of the island of Thera, which had been created by the Santorini volcano were plunged beneath the waves, when the underground lake of lava on which they rested suddenly emptied out. It is from volcanic explosions of this type, rather than from earthquakes, that we might get the picture of large areas of land suddenly being plunged deep into the sea.

The explosion of Krakatoa had a genuine doomsday air about it. It created huge tidal waves, which moved across the sea like fifty-foot-high walls of water, and crashed into nearby islands. All low-lying coastal towns in the path of the waves were swamped. Nearly thirty-seven thousand people were drowned by the waves. This death toll was exceptionally high because the ash cloud from the explosion was so thick that it blotted out the sun. In the darkness created by the cloud people could not see the waves coming and could make no attempt to save themselves.

The explosion threw so much volcanic dust high into the

air that it formed a huge cloud which circled the globe for two years, causing unusually brilliant sunsets and actually cutting down measurably on the amount of solar radiation reaching the earth. As a result, the temperatures throughout the world were depressed slightly for the two years following the explosion.

To the people of the neighboring islands the explosion of Krakatoa must have seemed like the end of the world. And to thousands it was indeed the end of their world. But the event, terrible and awesome as it was, inspired no general end-of-the-world panic.

The explosions of Krakatoa and Santorini were mere popguns compared to some volcanic explosions that took place in the past.

Large portions of the state of Oregon, northern California, and northwestern Nevada are covered by a type of rock called Mesa basalt. The total area of Mesa basalt has been estimated as at least 100,000 square miles. Drs. Harry E. Wheeler and Howard A. Coombs, geologists from the University of Washington believe, "At some time in the planet's rather recent past, Mesa basalt was squeezed up as a fiery liquid, or magma, which cooled and hardened after spreading over the surface." The "fairly recent past" here means anywhere from two to five million years ago.

The scientists are not sure whether this burning rock flowed from a single huge vent, or a series of closely connected vents, or whether the explosion lasted several months, or just a few days. Whatever the case, this huge sheet of volcanic rock, conservatively estimated at more than 350 cubic miles of material, must have been laid down in a short time by an awesome catastrophe.

Yet volcanoes should not inspire end-of-the-world fears. Catastrophic as they may seem, they are still local catastrophes, even if the "locality" is 100,000 square miles. They are neither omens nor agents of the end of the world.

The poet Robert Frost wrote:

> Some say the world will end in fire,
> Some say in ice . . .

The fire of the volcanoes has never inspired Western man's imagination to the extent that the ice of the glaciers has, at least over the last two centuries.

Men who lived in northern latitudes have always known about glaciers, gigantic frozen rivers which creep ever so slowly down from the regions of everlasting snow at the tops of mountains. As far as men knew the glaciers had always been there, impressive enough to be sure, but hardly anything to worry about. Then in the nineteenth century, men discovered the Ice Age.

The Ice Age should really have been suspected much earlier. For a long time partisans of catastrophic geological theories liked to point to erratics, huge boulders that obviously came from mountains but were found standing in the middle of flat plains, as proof of past catastrophes. Then there were the moraines, masses of smaller rocks that looked as though they had been pushed into a ridge by giant hands. Such geological oddities were attributed to whatever form of catastrophe the theorist pointing to them happened to favor.

A Swiss geologist named Horace Benedict de Saussure concluded that these geological oddities were the result of water and earthquakes: "There is no doubt at all that these stones were moved by water. . . . But where could such quantities of water have come from? What gave them such violent momentum?"

Saussure concluded that the oceans had once covered large portions of the earth up to the tops of the mountains.

Aerial view of the Cerro Negro Volcano, west-central Nicaragua, in action. *U.S. Geological Survey*

Then there were a series of powerful earthquakes which opened up gigantic holes in the earth's surface. "The waters rushed with frightful violence into these abysses; they carried with them enormous quantities of earth, sand, and fragmented stone. This great mass of water mingled with stone caused the depositing of the materials whose remnants we still see lying today."

But by the middle of the nineteenth century such mind-boggling catastrophic theories had lost their appeal. In 1848 a little-known German government official won a scientific prize for a three-volume work on the changes on the earth's surface. This official's name was Karl Ernst Adolf von Hoff of Gotha. Von Hoff was almost violently anticatastrophic: "Neither tradition nor the observation of nature offer proofs for a single or repeated upheaval or for the destruction of an entire organic creation."

In a remarkably farsighted sentence he wrote, "In the history of the globe it is not at all necessary to economize on time, but definitely on energy."

The story of Atlantis was in vogue at the time, just as it is today. Von Hoff analyzed it and dismissed it as a myth.

There was nothing very original or striking about Von Hoff's opposition to catastrophism in 1848 but it was an indication of how geological thinking had changed. His most important idea concerned the erratic boulders and the mysterious moraines. "Perhaps these fragments were transported in and on ice," he said.

In the years that followed many others arrived at the same idea. Men of science had come to the startling and unsettling realization that not so many thousands of years ago large portions of Europe, Asia, and North America had been covered by ice. The places where the cities of New York, London, and Berlin now stand had been under thick sheets of ice sixty thousand years ago, during what geologists call the Pleistocene epoch.

At first it seemed as though the geologists had merely discovered a new kind of catastrope, with ice replacing the water of the universal deluge. Even today catastrophic theorists like to believe that the Ice Age came on suddenly, almost overnight. They make much of the well-preserved remains of woolly mammoths found in the frozen ground of Siberia and Alaska. There are reports that the flesh of the great beasts is still fresh and that it could be served up at a banquet.

Immanuel Velikovsky, the twentieth century's leading catastrophist, points to these frozen carcasses and says that they could have remained in such an excellent state of preservation only if the animal had been trapped and frozen solid by a sudden and violent drop in temperature. "What could have caused such a sudden change in the temperature of the region?" Velikovsky asks. He then proceeds to answer the question with his own theories of recurrent cataclysms.

But, in fact, the frozen mammoths present no great puzzle. Russian scientists have shown how the mammoths could have been preserved by falling into deep crevasses. The carcasses at the bottom of the crevasses would be in the area of permafrost, that layer of ground in the northern latitudes which never thaws. Quickly, the dead mammoths would become covered with mud and snow from above. The mud would freeze, and the carcasses would be securely embedded in the permafrost. After thousands of years some of these carcasses have been revealed when the ground surrounding them has been stripped away by erosion or avalanche. No overnight catastrophic deep freezes need be brought in to account for the frozen mammoths. Besides, both the number and state of preservation of the mammoths is usually exag-

Midnight view of lava during the July, 1961 eruption of Kilauea Volcano in Hawaii. *U.S. Geological Survey*

gerated by those who like to see mysteries where there are none.

The Ice Age, scientists have determined, was not sudden, nor was it constant. The great ice sheets advanced and retreated repeatedly over a period of hundreds of thousands of years. There were an estimated five glacial and four interglacial periods in North America during the Pleistocene.

The Ice Age of the Pleistocene was not the only one in earth's history either. Geologists have found evidence that 500 million years ago, great blankets of cold and ice descended upon eastern Asia and the South Pacific region. Some 240 million years ago when primitive dinosaurs already inhabited inland seas an ice age covered India, Australia, South Africa, and South America. And there may well have been others.

Even if the advance of the ice was slow, any ice age represents a very dramatic change in the earth's climate. What can cause such changes? This is one of those questions, like the problem of the extinction of the dinosaurs, the existence of Atlantis, and the story of the Flood that has inspired practically everyone from distinguished professor to obsessed crank to come up with some sort of theory. Whole libraries have been written on the subject.

In 1920 Wilhelm Bölsche described the dilemma confronted by scientists who attacked the Ice Age problem: "Anyone who has had occasion to publish some findings about the Ice Age finds to his horror that innumerable manuscripts in terrifyingly bulky parcels collect on his desk, with and without return postage, whose senders invariably proclaim: I too have found a solution to the riddle of the Ice Age."

Currently the most popular scientific theory holds that the various ice ages were due to a complex interaction of astronomical and geological factors.

There is no need to go into a detailed history of the

great Ice Age controversy. Our primary concern is not what happened in the past, but what will happen in the future. The last major retreat of the glaciers in North America began about twenty thousand years ago. However, geologically speaking, we are still living in an ice age.

In his highly respected book *The World of Ice*, Professor James L. Dyson writes: ". . . the fact remains that the time in which we are living—an age of ice—is a most unusual period in the Earth's history. If the present were a normal period, the inhabitants of central Europe and the northern United States would probably be enjoying a subtropical climate."

He continues, "Most geologists believe that we are still in the ice age and many of them are of the opinion that vast sheets of ice will again spread over North America and Europe. There are some data to support this view, very few against it. . . . If the present is an interglacial stage comparable in length to several of the earlier ones, we are now somewhat less than halfway through it. If this be so, in another 10,000 to 15,000 years ice sheets will be on the move again. We know what they will do to the land—exactly what they have done in the past—but how will they treat mankind is an unanswered question and will depend a great deal upon man himself."

Physicist George Gamow is even more definite, "We must expect the ice that retreated some 10,000 years ago to come back again." He sets the date for return of the ice a little further in the future, some 20,000 years from now.

Will this apparently unavoidable glacial advance bring about the end of man's world? No! The ice will bring with it enormous worldwide changes in climate, but mankind should be able to survive these changes with relative ease. Our ancestors not only survived, but actually flourished during past ice ages, and they did so without central heating.

Today man inhabits land from the tropics to the tundra. A new ice age should hold no special terrors.

As the ice sheets push down across North America they will be preceded by vast shallow lakes, formed from the melting ice on the margins of the glaciers. Writes Professor Dyson: "There will be nothing catastrophic about the advance of the lake and ice across the prairies—the battle might go on for several thousand years. There will be places where large-scale agriculture will finally give way to small-scale subsistence farming, which in turn may yield to nomadism, and this perhaps eventually to the glaciers themselves. In his slow retreat before the glaciers and rising waters, man would fight them all the way. But against the ice it would be a losing battle until the glacier finally stopped its advance."

However, the effects of the advancing ice will be worldwide and they will not all be bad for man. "Not everywhere," writes Professor Dyson, "will Nature be unkind to man. The southward migration of the Polar Front and Prevailing Westerlies will bring more water to wet the world's arid desert lands. Each generation of ranchers and farmers in the western desert basins will have a little more irrigation water than the one before it. There will be more snow in the mountains and more rain in the basins . . .

"In the Sahara, in the great deserts of interior Asia, and in other vast dry regions the same changes will take place —more snow in the mountains, more rain in the lowlands. Lakes will expand and new ones will be born."

If it is not the violence of the earthquake, the fire of the volcano, or the ice of the glaciers, is there anything on or in the earth itself that is likely to bring about the end of mankind? The answer is probably no.

At one time the answer to that question would have been unhesitatingly no, for geology was dominated by the idea that all of the earth's processes were all slow and stately.

The well-preserved remains of a frozen baby woolly mammoth dug out of the frozen ground in Alaska. *Courtesy of the American Museum of Natural History*

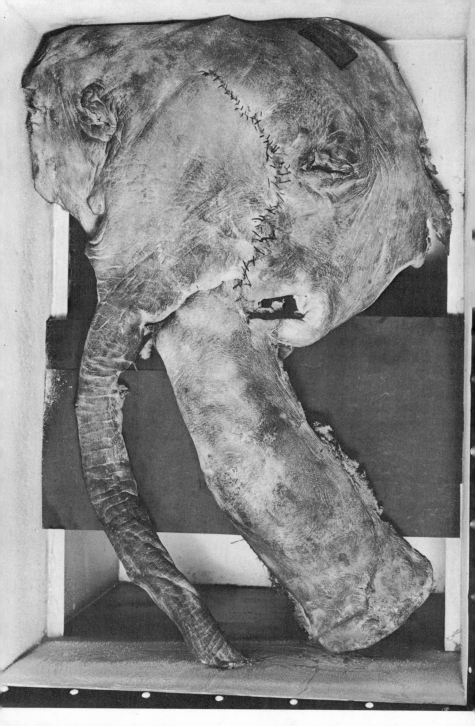

The noted geologist Haroun Tazieff has written, "Now the standard, recognized geology that we are taught at the university, and even by the professional experience that we subsequently gain in the field, is quite opposed to the doctrine of catastrophism. And it is all the more opposed to it because of the fact that not two hundred years ago the great natural philosophers would have nothing but catastrophism, and the reaction against their ideas, which was started and carried to its height in the nineteenth century, is still in force."

Tazieff is one of those geologists who believes that there have been more violent catastrophic events in earth's history than orthodox nineteenth-century geology would admit. What with new discoveries about the wobbling earth and the spreading sea floor, our planet no longer seems as stable as it once did.

But still, no responsible scientist believes that there were worldwide catastrophes on the level of the universal deluge, or anything envisioned by Cuvier and his followers. There has been no return to eighteenth-century catastrophism. Catastrophes, certainly, but local ones. If man can survive himself he will certainly be able to survive any such catastrophe.

What then is the future of the earth itself? There will, of course, be another glacial advance, but before that happens the earth should warm up for a few thousand years. According to George Gamow's estimate the warming-up of the Northern Hemisphere will continue for about the next twenty thousand years. "In the year 5000 the climate of Boston may resemble the present climate of Washington D.C.; in the year 10,000, that of the West Indies."

But then the ice will begin pushing out of the north, and the general warming process will be reversed. After a period of glaciation there will be another warming up period followed, about ninety thousand years from now by another advance of the glaciers.

This advance and retreat of the glaciers will continue monotonously as long as there are mountains. But there will not always be mountains. Mountains are formed by a crumbling of the earth's crust, brought about by changes deep within the earth's interior (perhaps influenced by a wobble in the earth's rotation). Geological evidence indicates that periods of mountain building occur on the earth about every 100 to 150 million years. There is no reason to believe that should change in the future. We are now living at the close of the Laramide Revolution, the period of mountain building that started in the time of the dinosaurs.

Some unknown millions of years from now this mountain building will cease entirely, and the mountains will slowly be washed away by the rains and other forces of erosion. The Rocky Mountains are high and spectacular because they are geologically young mountains. The Appalachian Mountains, on the other hand, are the worn-down stumps of much older mountains, and to a mountaineer they are hardly worth the name of mountain at all. But eventually both the Rockies and the Appalachians as well as the Alps, Andes, Himalayas, and all the other mountain chains in the world, great and small, will be worn away. The surface of the continents will become flat and boring and largely covered by marshlands and shallow seas.

But there will be a new period of activity deep beneath the earth's surface and another crumbling of the earth's crust. "Then," says Gamow, "new mountains will rise again, to the great enjoyment of alpinists; if there are any at that time."

There will be more glaciers, and finally the mountain building will end, and the mountains will be washed away. "And so on, and so on," says Gamow, "as long as the Sun remains shining in the sky."

And how long will that be? That, gentle reader, is the final problem that we will tackle.

CHAPTER 9

The Sun and the Moon

Yet the light of the bright world dies,
With the dying sun.
——FRANCIS WILLIAM BOURDILLON

The chances seem pretty good that our world will survive
the dangers of passing asteroids, nearby supernovas, and even
the unpredictable nature of man himself. But as we said in
the very beginning, the world is not eternal. It will come to
a certain and unavoidable end. The agents of destruction will
be either of the two most familiar objects in the sky, the sun
or the moon.

Since very ancient times the sun has been correctly regarded as the bringer of life to the world. The ancient Egyp-
tians worshiped the sun as Ra, their chief god. Most other
ancient peoples gave the sun god an equally prominent place
in their pantheons.

The Aztecs and other pre-Columbian Indians of Mexico
were obsessed with the sun. Each year they sacrificed thou-

sands of captives to insure that the sun would continue to rise every morning as it always had.

The Japanese regarded their emperor as a direct descendant of the sun itself. In Europe, as late as the seventeenth century, King Louis XIV of France was called the Sun King. He was the dazzling center about which all life in France was supposed to revolve.

In the middle of Salisbury Plain in England stands the gigantic ancient monument called Stonehenge. Though the purposes of this circle of huge stones are shrouded in mystery, at least one thing is clear, Stonehenge was used for the worship or observation of the sun, probably both. If an observer stands in the center of Stonehenge at dawn on midsummer's morning, the longest day of the year, he can look straight down the Avenue, an ancient roadway that leads to the monument, and watch the sun rise directly over the Heel Stone, the oldest and most significant stone in the entire monument. By this method the priests of Stonehenge could have kept track of the changing seasons.

No one in the ancient world was about to underestimate the importance of the sun.

The moon was of lesser importance. The gods, or often goddesses, of the moon were usually subordinate to the chief sun god. Sometimes the moon goddess was married off to the sun god. But as the second most obvious object in the sky, the moon could hardly be overlooked. The "pale moon" often was given a mysterious, slightly sinister connotation.

Both the sun and the moon are generally very regular and predictable. The sun rises at a known hour every morning and sets at a known hour every evening. The moon waxes and wanes on a regular schedule every month. To men of the ancient world there was only one unpredictable and spectacular thing that both the sun and the moon did—they became eclipsed every once in a while.

"Eclipses," writes Harvard astronomer Gerald Hawkins, "would clearly be among the most impressive and frightening natural phenomena that primitive men could encounter. What terror would strike the people as the god, or goddess, was swallowed up! Power and glory would surround the priest who could predict and thus seem to control those monstrous events. And vice versa—the famous story of the Chinese court astronomers Hsi and Ho who missed the solar eclipse of Oct. 22, 2137 B.C., and were promptly executed, may not be entirely true, but personally I would not like to have been the court astronomer of any country in any ancient time who failed to warn of a coming eclipse."

Dr. Hawkins believes that Stonehenge was not only a sun temple, but it was also sort of an ancient "computer" by which the priests were able to calculate the time that eclipses would occur. It was possible for people to predict eclipses, even if they did not understand what caused them. But such prediction would not have been easy and it would involve keeping records of eclipse observations over a long period of time. By moving a stone around some of the holes that are part of the Stonehenge complex Dr. Hawkins contends that the ancient Britons could have kept such records. Many archaeologists disagree. They doubt that the people who built the monument were sophisticated enough to use Stonehenge in the manner that Dr. Hawkins suggests.

But we do know that the astronomers of some ancient societies could predict both lunar and solar eclipses with great accuracy. The common people must surely have regarded such predictions as magic. The astronomers themselves, who were probably priests, would have encouraged this magical illusion and surrounded their doings with all

A solar eclipse photographed in 1970. *High Altitude Observatory, Boulder, Colorado*

sorts of occult mumbo jumbo. It would then appear that they possessed supernatural powers. In a way this sort of prediction really was magic. The astronomer-priests could do things that others could not. In a prescientific society, where is the dividing line between magic and science?

The Roman natural scientist Pliny (A.D. 23–79) asserted the predictions of eclipses was an ancient science, but:

"The most part of the common people have been and are of this opinion (received by tradition from their forefathers) that all the same is done by enchantments and that by the means of some sorceries and hearbes together, both sun and moon may be charmed, and enforced to loose and recover their light: To do which feat, women are thought to be more skilful and meet than men. And to say a truth, what a number of fabulous miracles are reported to have been wrought by Medea Queen of Colchis, and other women; and especially by Circe our famous witch here in Italy, who for her singular skill that way, was canonized a goddesse."

In some places it was traditional to make loud noises in order to frighten away the monster or demon who apparently had devoured the sun or moon.

There are numerous incidents where the occurrence of an eclipse profoundly altered the course of human events. One of the most famous occurred in 415 B.C., during an Athenian military expedition against the city of Syracuse in Sicily.

Nikias, commander of the Athenians, was at the point of withdrawing when an eclipse of the moon occurred. Nikias chose to regard this as an omen of ill fortune for his enemies, so he delayed his retreat. As a result he was defeated and lost both his fleet and his life. The Athenian expedition against Syracuse was transformed from a failure to a disaster.

Alexander the Great looked at a lunar eclipse on September 20, 331 B.C. He also chose to regard the eclipse as an

According to legend a solar eclipse occurred during a battle
between the Medes and the Persians in the fifth century B.C.
The terrified armies fled and the battle was never concluded.
Yerkes Observatory

A Chinese illustration depicting an eclipse as a solar dragon.
Yerkes Observatory

evil omen for his foes. Unlike Nikias, Alexander was right.
Eleven days later he defeated the Persian King Darius at the
decisive battle of Arbela.

There is a story that during one of his later voyages
Christopher Columbus was saved by a lunar eclipse. Columbus was at Jamaica and critically short of both food and water. The Indians had refused to help him obtain supplies. By
chance the admiral consulted an astronomical almanac which
listed the coming eclipses of the moon, and found one was
due that very night.

Columbus was then supposed to have invited the leading
Indians aboard his ship and warned them that God was very
angry because of their failure to aid his mariners. "As a sign
of His displeasure, He will this very evening take away the
moon from the sky as a clear token of the punishment to
follow, unless you bring food and water."

Columbus then withdrew to his cabin, and the eclipse began. The Indians became panic-stricken as the shadow of darkness extended across the face of the moon.

When the eclipse was nearly over, Columbus returned and announced "I have interceded with God on your behalf, and God has consented to take the shadow away." Naturally the Indians then gave Columbus and his men everything they wanted.

The story, however, does not really ring true. Lunar eclipses are common enough events. Though they certainly must have been regarded with fear and awe, the Indians must also have been familiar with them. They would not have been quick to believe that the eclipse was solely under the control of the newly arrived white man and his God. Who would have been responsible for the eclipses before Columbus arrived?

There is really nothing mysterious or dangerous about an eclipse. In an eclipse of the moon, the moon becomes obscured by passing into the dark shadow cast by the earth in space.

In an eclipse of the sun, the sun is concealed when the moon passes between the sun and the earth. An annular eclipse is a solar eclipse in which a ring of sunlight is visible around the dark moon. The entire sun is obscured in a total eclipse, when the moon is closer to the earth.

A total lunar eclipse occurs over any single spot on earth approximately once every 18½ years. A total solar eclipse occurs over any single spot on earth approximately once every 400 years. Lunar eclipses do not stimulate much excitement today, and most people won't even bother to get out of bed to see one. A solar eclipse, on the other hand, will still attract an enormous amount of attention. Astronomers will travel halfway around the world to get a good view of a total eclipse of the sun.

In those parts of the world where the real reasons for solar eclipses are still poorly understood the eclipse can, even today, be regarded as a powerful omen of doom. On February 4, 1962, more than 500,000 Hindu pilgrims plunged into the sacred Ganges River in India. They had come to wash away what they believed to be the evil effects of a solar eclipse.

But in the West it has been centuries since eclipses of either the sun or the moon have stirred extensive end-of-the-world fears.

While the earth is often shaken by earthquakes, volcanoes, and other natural phenomena, the sun and the moon seem unchanging and unchangeable. But they are not. What are the futures of the sun and moon, and how will they effect the future of the earth?

The origins of the moon are shrouded in obscurity and thus controversy. Scientists, however, have made some educated guesses at what the future of the moon will be.

The rotation of the earth on its axis is slowing. At the same time the moon is drawing away from the earth. None of this is happening very rapidly. Each day is about one two hundred millionths of a second (0.00000002) longer than the day before. Over a century the day is lengthened by only 0.00073 seconds. The moon is drawing away from the earth at the rate of about four inches a month. That means each new moon you see is approximately four inches farther away than the previous new moon. Considering that the mean distance of the moon from the earth is 238,857 miles, the moon is not really pulling away at breakneck speed. The lengthening of the day is also so minute that it has no practical effect on the earth, even over centuries. The lengthening of the day, however, has caused some minor mathematical problems for astronomers in the past. At one time astronomers

A woodcut printed in England in 1644 showing the supposed meaning of an eclipse, that occurred that year. The explanation reads, "Great Eclipse of the Sun Or Charles His Waine Overclouded by Evill Influences of the Moon, the malignancie of Ill-aspected Planets, and the Constellations of Retrograde and Irregular Starres. Otherwise, Great Charles, our Gracious King, eclipsed by the Seductive Perswasions of his Queen. . ." *New York Public Library Picture Collection*

regarded the earth as a perfect clock. But when the positions of the sun, moon, Mercury, and Venus were calculated in respect to the "fixed" stars they all seemed just slightly ahead of time, when they were compared to the calculations that had been made a century earlier. Either the earth was slowing down, or everything else was speeding up. The astronomers decided that the earth was slowing down. The total accumulated error over a century was a mere thirteen seconds, a small figure, "But it is well within the range of accuracy of astronomical observations and calculations," says physicist George Gamow.

The reason the earth is slowing down is because there are tides, caused mainly by the moon. The daily tides in the oceans around the world exert a slight braking action on the earth's rotation. The friction of the water against the sea bottom, the impact of the tidal waves on the shores of the continents, as well as the internal friction of the water itself all dissipate energy, and as a result the earth slows down ever so slightly.

Over a very long period of time the slowly accumulating effects of the slowing of the earth and recession of the moon might be very dramatic. At some point in the future the moon will be 20 percent farther away from earth than it is today. That will be its maximum distance from the earth. By that time the earthly day and the lunar month will be the same length, about fifty of our present days. The moon will hang immovably above one of the terrestrial hemispheres, and the lunar tides will cease.

But this will not be the final end of the moon. Though the lunar tides will have ended, there is still the influence of the sun to be accounted for, and the sun's pull too creates tides on the earth. The friction of the solar tides will continue to slow the earth's rotation, and ultimately the length of the earthly "day" will be equal to the length of a year.

The slowing of the earth's rotation to this extent will have horrifying effects on the earth itself. With one side of the planet facing the sun for such an extended period, the "day" side will become unbearably hot, while the "night" side will be frigid. Violent storms will rage where the hot air from the "day" side of the earth clashes with the cold air from the "night" side. Ultimately the surface of the earth may come to resemble the surface of Venus, which has a "day" that is 250 days long. On Venus the difference in temperature between "day" and "night" sides of the planet may be 700° F.

Another effect of this continued slowing is that the moon will not remain stable relative to the earth. Slowly it will be dragged back toward the earth.

The moon will return to the vicinity of the earth more slowly than it retreated because the force of the solar tides are much smaller than the force of the lunar tides. But as the moon comes ever closer to the earth the two bodies will exert an ever greater pull on one another. The lunar tides will return with a vengeance. At the point of its closest approach to the earth a towering permanent high tide will flood the lands under the moon leaving shores high and dry one quarter of the way around the globe.

One might expect that the whole moon will come crashing into the earth, but it won't. When the moon reaches a distance of about five thousand miles from the earth's surface it will fall within the Roche Limit. About a century ago a French astronomer named M. Roche calculated that any natural satellite that revolved around a planet at a distance of less than 2.5 times the planet's radius would break into pieces because of the gravitational forces. (Artificial satellites don't count, because being made entirely of metal they are much sturdier than natural satellites.)

The rings of Saturn may be examples of what happens to a moon that passes the Roche limit. Some think the rings are the remains of a satellite or satellites that got too close to the mother planet and broke up. Beyond the rings and the Roche limit, are nine moons of Saturn which orbit the planet without being broken to bits.

When our moon breaks up it will form a ring around the earth much like the rings around Saturn. We should then expect many uneventful eons in the relationship between earth and her former satellite. The tides will flatten out, and all will be quiet until some of the chunks of the ring begin moving in close enough to be pulled to the surface by the earth's gravitation. When that begins to happen the earth will be faced with a rain of destruction on an unparalleled scale. The chunks of the shattered moon will hit earth with far greater frequency than did the meteorites of the past.

We must stress that all of this about the retreat and ultimate return of the moon is entirely theoretical and controversial. This is speculation at the very limits of our scientific knowledge. Moon exploration will dramatically increase human knowledge about the history of the moon within a very few years, but at present we are still guessing about the moon's past and future.

In any event, the problem of what happens to the moon is an academic one, for there will be no men on earth to witness the breakup of our satellite, indeed there may be no moon and no earth either. Long, long before any of the catastrophic events created by the return of the moon can come to pass the earth will have become uninhabitable, and it may well have been destroyed completely. The recession and return of the moon will take many billions of years, and our sun has only another 5 billion years left to live.

Ironically we know more about the birth and death of stars like the sun than we know about the birth and death of planets and their satellites. Just looking up at the sky on a clear dark night we can see thousands of stars. With powerful telescopes astronomers can see millions of stars. But even with the most powerful telescopes now available, we cannot see any planets outside of our own solar system. Stars glow and are highly visible, planets don't glow and cannot be seen across the vast distance of interstellar space. Astronomers believe that they have located a planet orbiting a nearby star, but they can't actually see the planet itself. They have been able to detect a slight gravitational effect which the planet has on the star about which it presumably orbits.

We assume that many other stars are orbited by planets, like the planets in our own solar system, but we do not know for sure.

All the planets in our solar system were formed at the same time, they don't tell us much about past or future history. The stars we can see in various stages of evolution from birth to death. This gives astronomers a good chance to compare their theoretical predictions about the future of stars like the sun with the observed evolutionary stages of the various stars in the sky, and puts our knowledge about stars on a much sounder basis.

Stars are believed to form from clouds of hydrogen gas which surge and eddy through the vast reaches of interstellar space. Perhaps these clouds are the debris of stars long dead. We do not know. Sometimes during the random swirling of these thin clouds they form denser pockets of gas. Normally such pockets would disperse quickly, but if there is enough gas in a single pocket, the individual hydrogen atoms will exert enough gravitational pull on one another to hold the pocket together indefinitely. What is formed is a large and independent cloud of gas, much denser than the thin interstellar gas and quite identifiable to astronomers.

As time passes, the atoms of this cloud continue to exert a gravitational attraction upon one another, and they all begin to "fall" toward the center. The speed of the atoms increases, and this increase in energy raises the temperature of the shrinking gas cloud. Over a span of millions of years the gas cloud will have shrunk from a diameter of, say, 10 trillion miles to a diameter of a little less than a million miles, which is about the diameter of our sun. The sun is a very typical star. At this point the temperature at the center of the contracting gas ball reaches the critical value of 20 million degrees Fahrenheit.

The temperature and pressure at the center of this gas cloud, now properly called a star, are so great the protons or the nuclei of the hydrogen atoms, which formed the original cloud, are fused to form helium. This is a thermonuclear reaction and it releases an enormous amount of energy in the form of heat and light. The same sort of thermonuclear reaction takes place when a hydrogen bomb explodes, though obviously on a much smaller scale.

The energy released in this reaction is radiated to the surface of the star and then outward into space in the form of heat and light. Our sun looks like a huge burning ball of gas. But in truth the real "burning," that is, the thermonuclear reactions that power the sun, are taking place at the sun's center. While the center of the sun is 20 million degrees, its surface is only a few thousand degrees. About 10 percent of the solar matter surrounding the sun's core participates actively in energy production. The rest of the solar matter forms an outer mantle which is heated by the energy produced at the core. At the core of a star a small amount of matter can produce a great deal of energy. But such reactions can not go on forever. Sooner or later the "nuclear fuel" will be "burned up," and the star will die.

How long will this process take? The life span of a star depends on its size. Strangely, the larger the star the shorter its life. In a very large star the temperatures at the center are higher than 20 million degrees, and the thermonuclear reactions take place more quickly, and thus the star burns out more quickly. A star ten times as massive as the sun may live only 10 million years. At the other end of the scale a star one tenth the size of the sun, and that is about as

The disintegration of the moon as it approaches too closely to the earth, as imagined by artist Walter Favereau. The drawing was made for an "End of the World" show at the Hayden Planetarium. *Courtesy of the American Museum of Natural History*

small as a star can be, may continue "burning" slowly for a trillion years.

As we said the sun is an average-sized star, just about in the middle of the size-scale of known stars. The sun is "burning" quietly now. The sunspots and solar flares that appear so dramatically on the sun's surface seem to be part of the normal operation of the sun. We really can't explain these phenomena, and we know that they are violent enough to have effects, both far out in space and here on earth. Some people think that virtually everything from the weather to human history has been related in one way or another to sunspots. Most of these sunspot theories are about as valid as astrology. But neither sunspots nor solar flares seem capable of bringing about the end of the world, and their violence, spectacular as it may appear, is nothing compared to the violence that will accompany the death of the sun.

Our sun is now some 4.5 billion years old, and astronomers estimate that it has a total lifespan of 10 billion years. Thus the sun is a middle-aged star, about halfway through its anticipated life. In another 5 billion years or so the reserves of "nuclear fuel" at the sun's core will be exhausted, and the sun will begin to die.

It is only natural to think of the dying sun in the familiar terms of a dying fire. The flames flicker out slowly, leaving behind glowing embers which in time also darken and cool. The warmth and light that the fire threw out gradually grows less and less until it ceases entirely. Under such conditions one might imagine the sun growing dimmer and dimmer in the sky. Each year the amount of solar energy reaching the earth would be slightly less than the year before, and ultimately the temperature of earth would fall to the point where life no longer could be sustained. Then the world would truly end in ice.

A cloud of gas and dust in which stars are being born, situated about 4000 light years from the sun. Scattered throughout the area are small dark pockets of gas believed to be stars in the process of formation. *Mount Wilson and Palomar Observatories*

But stars don't die that way, and the end of our world is almost certainly fire and not ice. In about 5 billion years when the hydrogen at the sun's core is completely exhausted the "nuclear fire" will begin to spread to the outer layers of the sun which still contain "unburned" amounts of hydrogen. This will bring the thermonuclear reactions closer to the surface of the sun. The body of the sun will then begin to expand.

As the sun expands, its color will change from its present yellow-white to red. Such swollen and reddish stars are called *red giants*. A well-known example of a *red giant* is the star Betelgeuse, a fairly bright star in the constellation of Orion, which looks reddish even to the naked eye.

The transformation of the sun into a red giant will be very rapid from an astronomical point of view. It will take only 100 million years compared to the total lifespan of an estimated 10 billion years for the sun.

What is going to be happening on earth while the sun becomes a red giant? Rather than cooling off, the earth will be heating up. Though the surface temperature of the sun will be dropping it will be radiating more energy into space, and thus more solar energy will be hitting the earth. Just how fast the earth will heat up and how hot it will become is unknown, but at some point the oceans will boil away, and the surface of the earth will become red-hot. The atmosphere itself may evaporate into space.

There will, of course, be no one on the earth to observe the sun at this point, which is rather a pity. The sun will now be a magnificent sight, a red globe filling most of the sky.

As the sun expands it will swallow the inner planets of Mercury and Venus, and its surface will come close to the surface of the earth. Says George Gamow, "More detailed calculations than we have now are needed in order to predict whether the Sun will also swallow the Earth and will continue to expand toward Mars."

Says Harvard astronomer Dr. Carl Sagan, "One result of the evolution of our sun through the red giant phase will very likely be the reduction of our earth to a bleak, charred cinder."

This will indeed be the end of the world. However, if the earth is not engulfed by the expanding sun, there is an outside chance that it will experience a brief "rebirth."

Once the sun reaches its maximum size and all the reserves of hydrogen fuel are exhausted it will begin to shrink.

With its fuel gone the sun will no longer be able to generate processes needed to maintain itself against the tremendous forces of gravity. But as the sun collapses the pressures at the interior will again raise its temperature, ultimately to the critical level of 200 million degrees. The hydrogen which formed the sun's fuel during most of its lifespan will be gone, but the helium produced during 10 billion years will then become the now "nuclear fuel." At the critical temperature of 200 million degrees the helium nuclei are fused into carbon nuclei, and this releases more energy and rekindles the star. The duration of this stage in the life of the sun will be brief, about 100 million years. But at some point the collapsing sun will again reach its present size and brightness. If there is any atmosphere left on earth at that point the water that was boiled away will once again condense and refill the ocean basins, in the form of great rainstorms. For fifty million years or so, the earth may again be habitable and some new forms of life may evolve. But it won't last long. As the sun continues to shrink the earth will cool, and then become too cold to sustain life. The earth will be frozen, and there will be no chance of rewarming at this point.

The sun will keep burning until all its helium fuel is used up. It will then collapse once again, this time all its matter will be squeezed into a tiny space. The sun may, at this point be the size of the earth. It is estimated that in such a collapsed star the density is so great that a volume of matter the size of a matchbox will weigh ten tons. The surface of such stars glow white-hot, and they are called *white dwarfs.* The white-dwarf stage may last billions of years. During this white-dwarf phase the last of the star's energy is radiated out into space and, says Dr. Robert Jastrow of the Goddard Institute for Space Studies, "it fades into a blackened corpse."

That is the way in which the sun and the earth along

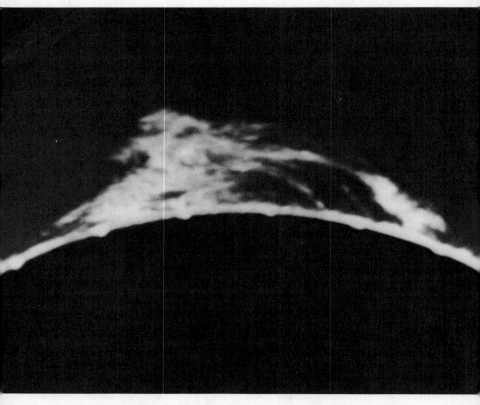

The surface of the sun. The solar flare or prominence is estimated to be some 132,000 miles high. *Mount Wilson and
Palomar Observatories*

with it probably will go. But there is also a possibility that the
ending for both may be a good deal more spectacular and
sudden. Dying stars are unstable and sometimes rather than
collapsing in an orderly manner they explode as nova or
supernova. As we pointed out in Chapter 6 such explosions
are not uncommon in the universe. Some astronomers once
believed that such explosions were an inevitable part of the
death of a star. But now it seems as if they are not.

The Indian astrophysicist S. Chandrasekhar carried out a detailed mathematical analysis of the theoretical inner structures of collapsed stars. His conclusion was that large stars explode while smaller stars continue to contract and expire quietly as white dwarfs. The dividing line between the two types of stars, called Chandrasekhar's Limit, is a body with a mass about 1.5 that of the sun. That places our sun a bit too near the dividing line for absolute comfort. Writes Robert Jastrow, "The sun happens to lie just below the dividing line, we are not certain which turn it will take at the end of its life, but we suspect that it will fade away."

George Gamow has also raised the possibility that the sun may explode because of external rather than internal causes. There are clouds of interstellar gas floating through space. Says Gamow, "If such a star, moving through space at a very great velocity, enters such a cloud of dilute material, it will burst into high luminosity in the very same way as does a meteorite that enters our terrestrial atmosphere, and, in fact, the kenetic energy of stellar motion, when thus transformed into heat, can easily supply the tremendous radiation characteristic of novae."

If the sun does explode, the heat will melt earth and all of the other planets of the solar system. Concludes Gamow: ". . . streams of hot gases emanating from the exploding Sun may even throw the molten planets clear out of the solar system. When the force of the explosion is spent what is left of the Sun and its planets will gradually cool to the temperature of interstellar space, which is hundreds of degrees below freezing."

But the possibilities of either type of explosion fortunately seem slim in the light of currently accepted theories. It is far more likely that our charred and frozen planet will wind up orbiting a cold dead sun.

So there we have it, the final cutoff date for the end of
the world is some 5 billion years from today. No cause for
immediate concern.

Where will man be when the world comes to an end? We
can only speculate, and the conclusions one arrives at depends
on whether one is an optimist or a pessimist. Dr. Jastrow is an
optimist. He suggests that man might well be able to witness
the swelling of our sun into a red giant and the scorching of
our home planet by the expanding sun. "Perhaps Jupiter will
be a suitable habitat for us by then. More likely, we will have
fled to another part of the Galaxy."

But other scientists suggest that well before the final end
of the world man will somehow have passed from the scene
and perhaps will have been replaced by something else.

Writes Gamow, "There is also no way of guessing which
breed of animals will take the throne of the 'Dictator of the
Earth', and we may well look with suspicion and rivalry at any
small creature that may now be crawling at our feet!"

Since the chapters of this book have been adorned with
quotes ranging from biblical to doggerel, it seems only fitting
that we should close with one. It is from the Book of Revelation (8:1) and describes one of the incidents in apocalyptic
vision attributed to St. John. It is one of the most enigmatic
and unsettling phrases in the entire Bible:

And when he had opened the seventh seal, there was
silence in heaven about the space of half an hour.

BIBLIOGRAPHY

BOOKS

Ardrey, Robert. *The Territorial Imperative.* New York: Atheneum, 1966.

Asimov, Isaac. *The Universe.* New York: Walker, 1966.

Berry, William B. N. *Growth of a Prehistoric Time Scale.* San Francisco: W. H. Freeman, 1968.

Bessy, Maurice. *A Pictorial History of Magic and the Supernatural.* London: Spring Books, 1964.

Bowman, John S. *The Quest for Atlantis.* New York: Doubleday, 1971.

Branston, Brian. *Gods of the North.* New York: Vanguard, n.d.

Brown, Hugh Auchencloss. *Cataclysms of the Earth.* New York: Twayne, 1967.

Carrington, Richard. *A Guide to Earth History.* London: Chatto & Windus, 1956.

Carson, Rachel. *Silent Spring.* Boston: Houghton Mifflin, 1962.

Cayce, Edgar Evans. *Edgar Cayce on Atlantis.* New York: Paperback Library, 1968.

Chaplin, J. P. *Rumor, Fear and the Madness of Crowds.* New York: Ballantine, 1964.

Cohen, Daniel. *The Age of Giant Mammals.* New York: Dodd, Mead, 1969.

————. *A Modern Look at Monsters*. New York: Dodd, Mead, 1970.

————. *Mysterious Places*. New York: Dodd, Mead, 1969.

————. *Myths of the Space Age*. New York: Dodd, Mead, 1967.

————. *Watchers in the Wild*. Boston: Little-Brown, 1971.

Colbert, Edwin H. *The Age of Reptiles*. New York: Norton, 1965.

————. *Dinosaurs: Their Discovery and Their World*. New York: Dutton, 1961.

————. *Man and Dinosaurs*. New York: Dutton, 1968.

Curtis, Richard, and Hogan, Elizabeth. *Perils of the Peaceful Atom*. New York: Ballantine, 1970.

De Bell, Garrett (ed.). *The Environmental Handbook*. New York: Ballantine, 1970.

De Camp, L. Sprague. *Lost Continents*. New York: Dover, 1970.

————. and De Camp, Catherine Crook. *The Day of the Dinosaur*. New York: Doubleday, 1968.

————. and Ley, Willy. *Lands Beyond*. New York: Rinehart, 1952.

De Grazia, Alfred (ed.). *The Velikovsky Affair*. New York: University Books, 1966.

Donnelly, Ignatius. *Atlantis the Antediluvian World* (revised edition). New York: Grammercy, 1949.

Dyson, James L. *The World of Ice*. New York: Knopf, 1962.

Ehrlich, Paul R. *The Population Bomb*. New York: Ballantine, 1968.

Engle, Eloise. *Earthquake, the Story of Alaska's Good Friday Disaster*. New York: John Day, 1966.

Festinger, Leon; Riecken, Henry W.; and Schachter, Stanley. *When Prophecy Fails*. Minneapolis: U. of Minnesota Press, 1956.

Gamow, George. *A Planet Called Earth*. New York: Viking, 1963.

————. *A Star Called the Sun*. New York: Viking, 1964.

Gardner, Martin. *Fads and Fallacies in the Name of Science*. New York: Dover, 1957.

Gay, Peter. *The Enlightenment, an Interpretation, Vol. II*. New York: Knopf, 1969.

Gentry, Curt. *The Last Days of the Late, Great State of California*. New York: Putnam's, 1968.

Graham, Frank Jr. *Since Silent Spring*. New York: Consumers Union Edition, 1969.

Grant, Robert M. *Augustus to Constantine*. New York: Harper and Row, 1970.

Gordon, Theodore. *Ideas in Conflict*. New York: St. Martins, 1966.

Hamilton, Edith. *Mythology*. New York: Mentor, 1953.

Hawkins, Gerald S. *Meteors, Comets and Meteorites*. New York: McGraw-Hill, 1964.

———. *Stonehenge Decoded*. New York: Doubleday, 1965.

Heidel, Alexander. *The Gilgamesh Epic and Old Testament Parallels*. Chicago: U. of Chicago Press, 1949.

Hooker, Dolph Earl. *Those Astounding Ice Ages*. New York: Exposition, 1958.

Jastrow, Robert. *Red Giants and White Dwarfs*. New York: Harper and Row, 1967.

Jones, Gwyn. *A History of the Vikings*. New York: Oxford University Press, 1968.

Kummel, Bernhard. *History of the Earth* (second edition). San Francisco: W. H. Freeman, 1970.

Lane, Frank W. *The Elements Rage*. Philadelphia: Chilton, 1965.

LaPaz, Lincoln, and LaPaz, Jean. *Space Nomads*. New York: Holiday House, 1961.

Larousse Encyclopedia of Mythology. London: Paul Hamlyn, 1959.

Ley, Willy. *Another Look at Atlantis and Fifteen Other Essays*. New York: Doubleday, 1969.

———. *The Dawn of Zoology*. Englewood Cliffs, N.J.: Prentice-Hall, 1968.

———. *Visitors From Afar, the Comets*. New York: McGraw-Hill, 1969.

———. *Watchers of the Skies*. New York: Viking, 1963.

Mackay, Charles. *Extraordinary Popular Delusions and the Madness of Crowds*. Boston: L. C. Page, 1932.

Martin, P. S., and Wright, H. E. (eds.). *Pleistocene Extinctions, The Search for a Cause*. New Haven: Yale University Press, 1967.

Marx, Wesley. *The Frail Ocean*. New York: Ballantine, 1967.

Mavor, James W. Jr. *Voyage to Atlantis*. New York: Putnam's, 1969.

Moore, Ruth. *The Earth We Live On*. New York: Knopf, 1956.

Morris, Desmond. *The Naked Ape*. New York: McGraw-Hill, 1967.

Newall, R. S. *Stonehenge*. London: H. M. Stationery Office, 1966.

Nichol, Francis D. *The Midnight Cry*. Review and Herald Publishing Association. Takoma Park, Washington, D.C., 1944.

Osborn, Robert. *Mankind May Never Make It*. Greenwich, Conn.: N.Y. Graphic Society, 1968.

Paddock, William, and Paddock, Paul. *Famine—1975!* Boston: Little-Brown, 1969.

Perry, John. *Our Polluted World, Can Man Survive?* New York: Franklin Watts, 1967.

Rackham, Arthur. *The Arthur Rackham Fairy Book*. Philadelphia: Lippincott, n.d.

Rienow, Robert, and Rienow, Leona Train. *Moment in the Sun*. New York: Ballantine, 1967.

Rubowsky, John. *Life and Death of the Sun*. New York: Basic Books, 1964.

Sagen, Carl, and Shklovskii, I. S. *Intelligent Life in the Universe*. San Francisco: Holden-Day, 1966.

Sears, Clara Endicott. *Days of Delusion, A Strange Bit of History*. Boston: Houghton-Mifflin, 1924.

Shurcliff, William A. *S/S/T and Sonic Boom Handbook*. New York: Ballantine, 1970.

Silverberg, Robert. *Mammoths, Mastodons and Man*. New York: McGraw-Hill, 1970.

Simak, Clifford D. *The Solar System, Our New Front Yard*. New York: St. Martins, 1962.

Spence, Lewis. *The Problem of Atlantis*. New York: Brentano's, 1925.

Stearn, Jess. *Edgar Cayce: The Sleeping Prophet*. New York: Doubleday, 1967.

Sugrue, Thomas. *There is a River*. New York: Henry Holt, 1942.

Sullivan, Walter. *Assault on the Unknown*. New York: McGraw-Hill, 1961.

———. *We Are Not Alone*. New York: McGraw-Hill, 1964.

Tazieff, Haroun. *When the Earth Trembles*. New York: Harcourt, Brace and World, 1962.

Velikovsky, Immanuel. *Ages in Chaos*. New York: Doubleday, 1952.

———. *Earth in Upheaval*. New York: Doubleday, 1955.

———. *Worlds in Collision*. New York: Doubleday, 1950.

Wendt, Herbert. *Before the Deluge*. New York: Doubleday, 1968.

———. *Out of Noah's Ark*. London: Weidenfeld and Nicholson, 1959.

Widener, Don. *Timetable for Disaster*. Los Angeles: Nash, 1970.
Winks, Robin W. (ed.). *The Historian as Detective, Essays on Evidence*. New York: Harper and Row, 1969.
Woodbury, David O. *When the Ice Came*. New York: Dodd, Mead, 1963.
Woolley, Leonard. *Ur of the Chaldees*. London: Ernest Benn, 1929.
Young, Jean I. (translation and ed.). *The Prose Edda of Snorri Sturluson*. Berkeley: U. of California Press, 1964.

ARTICLES

Anthony, H. E. "Nature's Deep Freeze," *Natural History* (Sept. 1949).
Berry, James R. "What's Happening to Our World?" *Science Digest* (June 1968).
Cohen, Daniel. "The Great Dinosaur Disaster," *Science Digest* (March 1969).
Cox, Allan. "Reversals of the Earth's Magnetic Field," *Scientific American* (Feb. 1967).
Ehrlich, Paul. "Echo-catastrophe," *Ramparts* (Sept. 1969).
———. "People Pollution," *Audubon* (May 1970).
Frisch, Bruce. "Dandridge Cole: G.E.'s Way Out Man," *Science Digest* (July, 1965).
———. "Here Comes Icarus," *Science Digest* (June 1969).
Graham, Frank Jr. "Tempest in a Nuclear Teapot," *Audubon* (March 1970).
Heirtzler, J. R. "Sea Floor Spreading," *Scientific American* (Dec. 1968).
"How to Predict an Earthquake," *Saturday Review* (Oct. 5, 1968).
Hurley, Patrick M. "The Confirmation of Continental Drift," *Scientific American* (April 1968).
Newell, Norman D. "Crisis in the History of Life," *Scientific American* (Feb. 1963).
Purrett, Louise. "When the North Pole Goes South," *Science News* (April 10, 1971).
Richter, Charles F. "Earthquakes," *Natural History* (Dec. 1969).
Robert, Steven V. "Warning California Will Fall Into the Ocean in April," *The New York Times Magazine* (April 6, 1969).

Ternes, Alan P. (ed.). "The State of the Species," *Natural History* (Jan. 1970).

Terry, K. D., and Tucker W. H. "Biologic Effects of Supernovae," *Science* (Jan. 26, 1968).

Thorarinsson, Sigudur. "Hellfire," *Natural History* (August-Sept. 1971).

Tufty, Barbara. "Building to a Quake?" *Science News* (June 10, 1967).

Wheeler, Harry G., and Coombs, Howard. "100,000 Square Miles of Burning Rock," *The Saturday Review* (Oct. 5, 1968).

Index

INDEX 253

Ehrlich, Dr. Paul, 177–178, 185
Elements of Rage, 120
Eliot, T. S., 185
Ensisheim, 113
Ephesus, 112
Euphrates, 58–59, 61, 69
Exeter, New Hampshire, 28–29

Famine, 174–175
Faults, 189, 192; San Andreas, 189, 192, 196–197
Fenrir, 37
Fimbulvetr, 37, 41
French Academy, 113–114

Galilei, Galileo, 62
Gamov, George, 217, 220–221, 231, 243–244
General Electric Corporation, 173
Gentry, Curt, 193
Germany, 98; Berlin, 213
Gilgamesh Epic, 58
Gnosticism, 47
Goddard Institute for Space Statistics, 241
Graff, Henry F., 51
Greece, 78
Greenland, 42

Halley, Edmund, 93
Hamilton, Edith, 41
Harrison, Dr. E. R., 135, 138–139
Harvard Observatory, 115, 134
Hawkins, Dr. Gerald, 134, 224
Hays, Dr. James D., 161
Heimdall, 38, 40
Heirtzler, Dr. James R., 199
Herodotus, 111
Himes, Joshua V., 17–18, 28

Hindus, 82–83
Hittites, 111
Hollow Men, 185

Iacopi, Robert, 192
Ice Age, 156, 210, 213, 216–217
Iceland, 36, 206
India, 8, 112, 175
Indochina, 55
Indonesia, 8, 175
Inquisition, 62
Institute of Meteorites, University of New Mexico, 105
Iraq, 58
Ireland, 83
Italy, 226; Syracuse, Sicily, 226

Jamaica, 228
Japan, 80, 198; Hiroshima, 152, 165, 168; Nagasaki, 152, 165, 168
Jastrow, Dr. Robert, 241, 243–244
Jefferson, Thomas, 67, 113
Jehovah's Witnesses, 33
Jerusalem, 49–50, 89
John of Toledo, 54
Jones, Gwyn, 37
Josephus, 90
Journal of Geophysical Research, 199
Judea, 49
Judgement Day (Second Advent, Second Coming), 15, 17, 22–25, 29, 33, 35–36, 46, 49, 92, 166, 179
Julius Caesar, 90

Kennett, Dr. James P., 162
Kepler, Johannes, 151